FRONTIER
Pistols and Revolvers

This edition published by
CHARTWELL BOOK
A division of BOOK SALES, Inc
114 Northfield Avenue
Edison, New Jersey 08837
First English language edition, 1996
© Copyright, Paris, 1996

ISBN : 0-7858-0749-7

Printed in Spain

THE WORLD OF ARMS

FRONTIER
PISTOLS AND REVOLVERS

Dominique VENNER

CHARTWELL
BOOKS, INC.

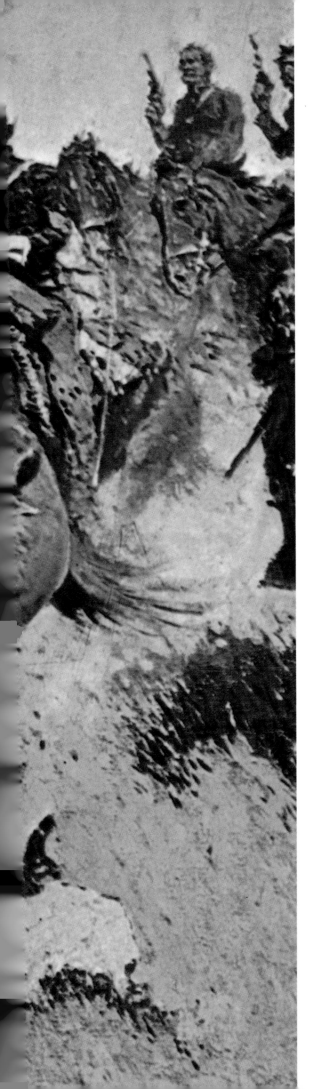

CONTENTS

Confederate cavalrymen at full gallop on the scorched plains of the West, revolvers in hand.

FIREARMS, AN AMERICAN HISTORY

The Mayflower.

Abraham Lincoln, sixteenth President of the
United States (1861-1865), with his son Tad.

America's attachment to firearms goes back to the pilgrims. In the seventeenth century, after an interminable crossing in unseaworthy ships, the first settlers landed in an unknown and inhospitable land, with only their flintlocks to protect them. Unlike the French colonists in Canada, the founders of New England did not make friends with the indigenous population, and after the first few encounters, relations with the Native Americans quickly soured. Bible in one hand, musket in the other, the *Mayflower* puritans and their successors fervently believed that they were the newly elected people of God, for whom the New World was destined for all eternity. They nourished an aversion and a contempt for the natives, whom they thought of as pagan "savages."

At first, the Native Americans felt no ill will toward the white settlers, and when asked to mark an X on a pile of incomprehensible papers, they did so obligingly. Later, the consequences of this strange game became clear to them, and when the whites declared that these "treaties" gave them legal title to their ancient tribal lands, the tribes rebelled. Blood ran on both sides. The colonists became more numerous and more aggressive. In 1662, the massacre of English colonists in Virginia was followed by an even bloodier reprisal. In 1675, fifty years after the arrival of the *Mayflower*, the chief of the Wampanoags, the now-extinct great tribe of the Atlantic Coast, assembled his warriors to chase out the invader. This first Indian war was the bloodiest of all: 20,000 Indians armed with bows and arrows against 50,000 settlers equipped with muskets and steel swords. The Indians were crushed. Their chief, "King Philip" as he was called by the English, was killed, and the survivors were deported to the West Indies and sold as slaves. This first Indian war set the stage for all the wars that followed over the next two centuries.

Native Americans were not the only enemies facing the English colonists in New York, Baltimore, and Philadelphia. They were also forced to fight against the French Canadians to the north, a cruel war that lasted a century and ended with the defeat of the Marquis de Montcalm under the walls of Quebec in 1759. Four years later the victory of the English colonies (and of England) was complete, and with the Treaty of Paris, France gave up all claims of sovereignty in what had until then been called New France.

This war was followed by the War of Independence (1775-1782), fought between England and its rebellious colonies, and the subsequent founding of the United States of America. The militia organized by the rebel colonies and supported by France, who thus avenged itself for the Treaty of Paris and the loss of Canada, took on and defeated His Majesty's regiments.

In the eighteenth century, the independent colonies, now the United States of America, continued to expand by opening their gates to an uninterrupted flow of European immigrants. In order to secure the territory that would later become the state of Texas, the settlers had to fight long and hard against both Native Americans and the Mexican army. Among them were the two heroes of the Alamo (1836), Davy Crockett and Jim Bowie. To conquer and create what they believed to be a land of liberty—the land of the Americans— they, like their predecessors, took up their arms and waged war—not as soldiers defending a state, but as free citizens of an independent republic.

The first immigrants going to church. The men are armed with muskets to protect their families against dangers of all kinds.

On April 9, 1865, after a war lasting four years, Robert E. Lee, General in chief of the Confederate armies, signed the South's surrender.

Jesse James aged 17.

Bud Ledbetter, Sheriff of Oklahoma and Arkansas from 1880 to 1896.

Personal firearms were indispensable in the wide open West, where not just Native Americans but Nature herself seemed to resist the pioneers and outlaws as they pushed the frontier all the way to the Pacific. A gun was necessary to combat mortal fear and mortal men—the worst predators in a time when the only law was, as the saying went, "Colt's law." Over the course of three centuries, America was built by the brave initiative of the individual, rifle in one hand, revolver in the other.

At the beginning of the seventeenth century, the first colonists in Virginia brought with them the European convention of their day, which held that only gentleman had the right to bear arms. Only 54 of the first 107 settlers met this distinction and were allowed to possess a firearm. Necessity prevailed, however, and this restriction was soon abandoned; in the four years following their arrival, all settlers would be given their own guns.

A new conception of civic responsibility had taken root here, one born of necessity but also tied to the ancient Celtic and Germanic concepts of the free man distinguished above all by his right and responsibility to bear arms.

After the great Indian revolt and massacre of 1662, the first Virginia militia conscripted all males between the ages of 16 and 50. The opposite of a regular army, the militia was composed of every farmer, worker, and townsman with a gun, who would be ready at any moment to respond to the raising of an alarm. The other colonies soon followed Virginia's lead and established their own militia.

After the War of Independence (1775-1782), the Second Amendment of the U.S. Constitution solemnly declared that "a well-regulated militia being necessary to the security of a free state, the right of the people to keep and bear arms shall not be infringed."

When the California gold rush hit in 1848, everyone wanted a pistol or, better still, a revolver, whose invention corresponded to the conquest of the West. A revolver carried in the belt or pocket left hands free to work or ride a horse. Ever present, ever ready, it provided, above all, comfort to a man in solitude—a pioneer's all-risk insurance plan, his "equalizer."

A hard-won philosophy was forged in the West. If in the hand of a criminal a gun is a threat, in the hand of a responsible citizen it is the means to stand up to that threat. A gun is the only defense against the misuse of a gun and therefore an invaluable instrument of justice and fair play.

The logic of this basic code is indisputable. From 1865 to 1900 there were only 600 murders in the West, while in New York, where the court system ruled, 1886 alone saw 799 murders. In reality, the bloody reputation of the West was the invention of the journalists of the period and the filmmakers of today. With so many armed men, the West was much more peaceful than the industrial towns. There is also a practical reason for the low murder rate. Contrary to the legend peddled by westerns, it is not easy to shoot a man with a revolver unless at point-blank range. The extravagant performances of marksmen in the movies happened only ... in the movies. Strongly influenced by the presence of numerous Confederate veterans—now cowboys—the unwritten code of the West was this: never shoot an unarmed man. All adversaries should be given the chance to draw first. A man who broke this code of honor exposed himself to immediate reprisals by the friends and family of the victim, or even by eyewitnesses. The nostalgia for this rugged epoch is felt everywhere today, not only in America. It explains why there is such a craze for old revolvers, the witnesses and symbols of more free and proud times.

A caravan of gold and silver miners on the road to Leadville, Colorado, in 1870.

SAMUEL COLT AND THE MODERN REVOLVER

The story of Samuel Colt is an American fairy tale come true. Born into a poor family on July 19, 1814, in Hartford, Connecticut, by the time of his death, he had amassed an immense fortune, achieved worldwide fame, and his name had become synonymous with the revolver. Contrary to legend, Sam Colt did not invent the revolver but capitalized on the technical inventions of his time to produce the first reliable and easy-to-use revolver. Not only was Colt knowledgeable about industrial progress, he was a shrewd businessman.

According to Sam Colt, the idea for the cylinder mechanism that made his fortune came in a flash of inspiration he had while looking at the hooking system on the helm of a sailing ship bound for India. Colt was fiftteen years old at the time. When he returned to America, he went to work for a gunsmith and developed his first prototype. In 1836, he registered his U.S. patent and started his first company in Paterson, New Jersey, where he manufactured the Colt Paterson revolvers.

Sam was able to sell his guns because of his boldness and intelligence. Hoping to get an order for his guns from the army, Colt went to Washington to present President Andrew Jackson with a specially engraved model and to dine with army officers. But the army was not interested in his revolvers. Colt then went to try his luck in the newly independent state of Texas. Though Texas became his first major client, sales remained low and the company went bankrupt in 1842. In 1847, Colt's luck changed when, thanks to a Colt admirer, Captain Sam Walker, the army put in an order for the war against Mexico. Production started up and never stopped again. The great adventure had begun.

11

Colt model 1848 Dragoon No. 1. This indefatigable revolver stayed in use in the West for a long time after the appearance of the first metal-case cartridge guns. It is not surprising, therefore, to see it next to a Winchester 1873 carbine.

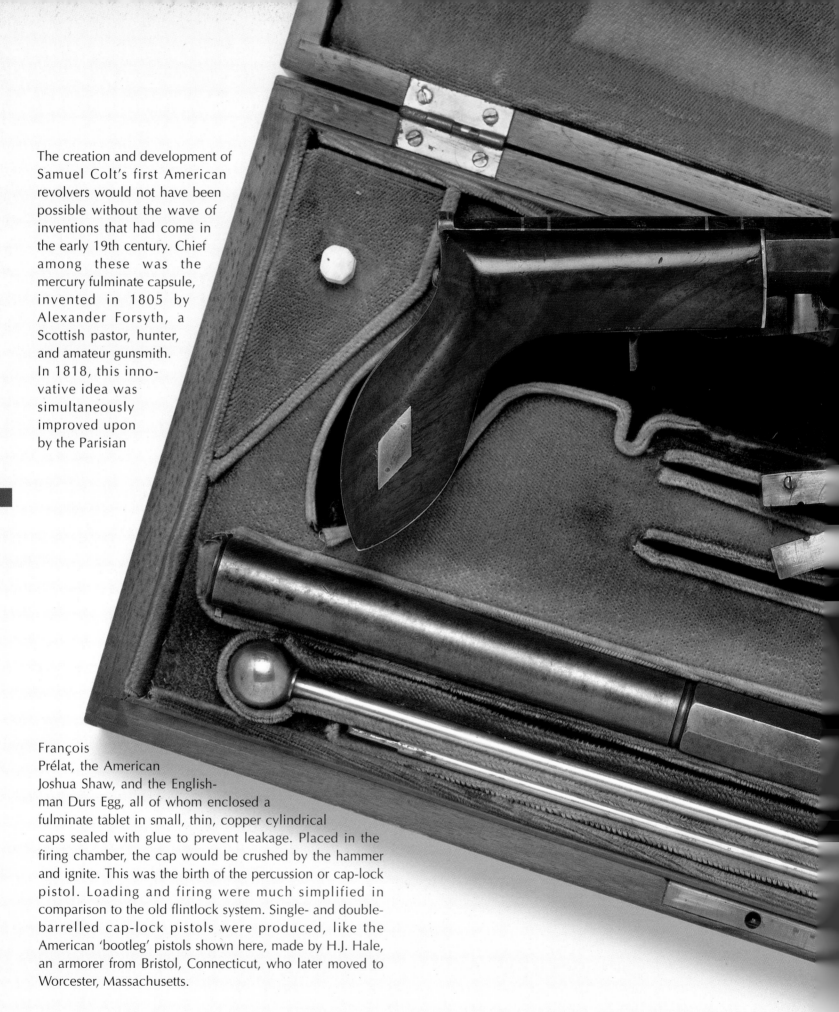

The creation and development of Samuel Colt's first American revolvers would not have been possible without the wave of inventions that had come in the early 19th century. Chief among these was the mercury fulminate capsule, invented in 1805 by Alexander Forsyth, a Scottish pastor, hunter, and amateur gunsmith. In 1818, this innovative idea was simultaneously improved upon by the Parisian

François Prélat, the American Joshua Shaw, and the Englishman Durs Egg, all of whom enclosed a fulminate tablet in small, thin, copper cylindrical caps sealed with glue to prevent leakage. Placed in the firing chamber, the cap would be crushed by the hammer and ignite. This was the birth of the percussion or cap-lock pistol. Loading and firing were much simplified in comparison to the old flintlock system. Single- and double-barrelled cap-lock pistols were produced, like the American 'bootleg' pistols shown here, made by H.J. Hale, an armorer from Bristol, Connecticut, who later moved to Worcester, Massachusetts.

H.J. Hale
"Underhammer"
pistols.
Manufactured in
Bristol, Connecticut.
Patented in 1835.
Firing system:
percussion cap lock.
Muzzle loaded.
.31 and .44 caliber.
Single shot.
6-inch partially
octagonal barrel.

The invention of the fulminate cap paved the way for the pepperbox, the ancestor of the revolver, which first appeared in 1820. Pepperboxes are composed of several barrels clustered around an axis pin. In the very first models the barrels had to be manually rotated in exactly the same way as you grind a peppermill—hence the name. The first Colt Paterson, which appeared in 1836, had four advantages over this crude system. Unlike a pepperbox, the Colt Paterson possesses a multi-chambered short cylinder in front of a single barrel, making it lighter, better balanced, and easier to handle. The manual cocking of the hammer (single action) rotates the cylinder until a chamber lines up exactly with the barrel. The cocking of the hammer also automatically engages the cylinder's locking mechanism and causes the folding trigger to swing down out of the frame automatically. The ramparts separating the firing chambers prevent 'chain-firing'—when the flash from an exploding fulminate cap radiates across the front of the cylinder and ignites some or all of the other chambers simultaneously.

Colt Paterson Belt Model.
Manufactured in Paterson, New Jersey, from 1837 to 1841.
Quantity manufactured: 2,700.
Firing system: percussion cap lock.
Chamber loaded.
Single action, sheathed trigger.
.31 caliber (also exists in .36 caliber).
Five-shot.
5-inch barrel.

Colt bullet mold.

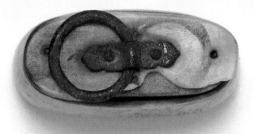

Snuffbox from the period.

Whiskey flask from the period.

SAMUEL COLT
AND THE MODERN REVOLVER

Colt Walker model Army 1847.
Manufactured in Whitneyville in 1847.
Quantity manufactured: 1,100.
Firing system: percussion cap lock.
Chamber loaded.
Single action, fixed trigger.
.44 caliber.
Six-shot.
9-inch barrel.
Weight: 4 pounds, 10 ounces (unloaded).

American powder horn.

Despite his efforts to sell Paterson revolvers, Samuel Colt went bankrupt in 1842. He managed to hold on until 1847, when a fortunate break came his way: the war between the United States and Mexico. Suddenly, the American army needed arms. Captain Sam Walker, who had much admired the first Colt revolvers, obtained an army order and suggested several improvements that were immediately adopted by the inventor. Samuel Colt started afresh, establishing a new company in New York and manufacturing the new revolver at the Whitney

factory in
Whitneyville.
The new model was
named after Captain Walker,
who was killed in the initial clashes
against the Mexicans. The .44-caliber
revolver, which uses a big half-ounce
conical bullet, was much heavier, more
solid, and bulkier than the Paterson.
While the Paterson was composed of
seventeenth pieces, the Colt Walker had
only five. The Colt Walker was equipped with
a fixed trigger protected by a brass trigger guard.
The open frame had a shield to protect the caps, with an
indentation for loading. A bullet reloader was fixed to the
console. The Colt Walker was manufactured for one year.

The Colt model 1848 Army Dragoon No.1 is not as big as the Colt Walker. The grip is brass plated; the cylinder is shorter. Oval notches (different from the following models) assure the cylinder-locking system. The rammer is fixed to the end of the barrel with a small bolt. The main V-shaped spring is the same as the one in the Walker.

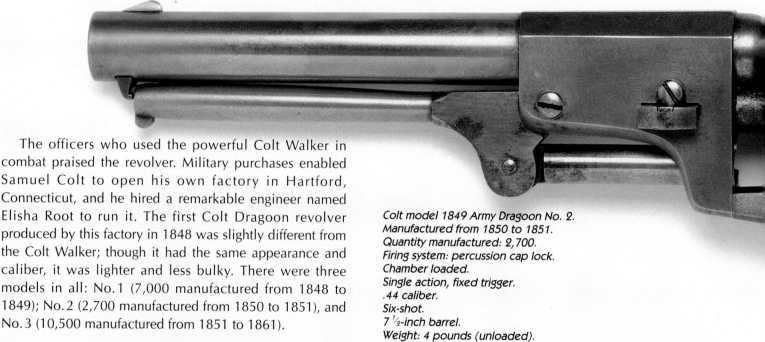

Colt model 1848 Army Dragoon No. 1.
Manufactured in Hartford, Connecticut, from 1848 to 1849.
Quantity manufactured: 7,000.
Firing system: percussion cap lock.
Chamber loaded.
Single action, fixed trigger.
.44 caliber.
Six-shot.
7 1/2-inch barrel.
Weight: 4 pounds (unloaded).

The officers who used the powerful Colt Walker in combat praised the revolver. Military purchases enabled Samuel Colt to open his own factory in Hartford, Connecticut, and he hired a remarkable engineer named Elisha Root to run it. The first Colt Dragoon revolver produced by this factory in 1848 was slightly different from the Colt Walker; though it had the same appearance and caliber, it was lighter and less bulky. There were three models in all: No.1 (7,000 manufactured from 1848 to 1849); No.2 (2,700 manufactured from 1850 to 1851), and No.3 (10,500 manufactured from 1851 to 1861).

Colt model 1849 Army Dragoon No. 2.
Manufactured from 1850 to 1851.
Quantity manufactured: 2,700.
Firing system: percussion cap lock.
Chamber loaded.
Single action, fixed trigger.
.44 caliber.
Six-shot.
7 1/2-inch barrel.
Weight: 4 pounds (unloaded).

Externally, the Colt model 1849 Army Dragoon No. 2 differs from the Dragoon No. 1 by the rectangular notches on the cylinder. The old V-shaped main spring was replaced by a straight spring. The hammer is pushed down onto this spring by means of a roller. The Colt revolver mechanism based on this model remained unchanged (except for the Root) until the famous 1873 Army Peacemaker, with its square-backed trigger guard.

Frederick Remington, creator of this etching, is one of the most famous artists inspired by the western epic. From 1886 until his death in 1909, he crossed the plains of the West, working as a cowboy in Montana, Wyoming, Arizona, and in both Dakotas. On horseback, with a lasso or Colt in his hand, he was one of the best. The way of life that he experienced for a long time—and which he represented in his drawings, etchings, paintings, and sculptures—gave his work a uniquely authentic style. In his drawings of horses, Indians, cowboys, or cavalrymen, his personal touch is immediately recognizable. There is an energy and a boldness to his work that can be found with no other artist. Arms are always represented or suggested with realism as in this scene of the arrest of an Indian by two cavalrymen.

The Colt model 1851 Dragoon No. 3 was identical to the Dragoon No. 2 except that the trigger guard was round instead of square-backed. King Victor-Emmanuel III, the architect of Italian national unity, was one of the famous users of this model. Approximately 9,500 were manufactured between 1851 and 1861. The model shown in the photograph is a very rare Dragoon No. 3½, which was designed to be used with an attachable shoulder butt, converting it into a short rifle. Notches on the frame and grip and two screws mounted in relief at the back of the frame hold the shoulder butt in place. A rear-sight adjuster soldered to the barrel console gives greater precision in long-distance shooting. Only 950 No. 3½ were manufactured between 1858 and 1860. Only collectors distinguish between the No. 3 and the No. 3½.

Colt model 1851 Army Dragoon No. 3 ½.
Manufactured in Hartford, Connecticut, from 1858 to 1860.
Quantity manufactured: 950.
Firing system: percussion cap lock.
Chamber loaded.
Single action, fixed trigger.
.44 caliber.
Six-shot.
7 ½-inch barrel.
Weight: 4 pounds, 2 ounces (unloaded).

Shoulder butt from a Colt Dragoon No. 3 ½.

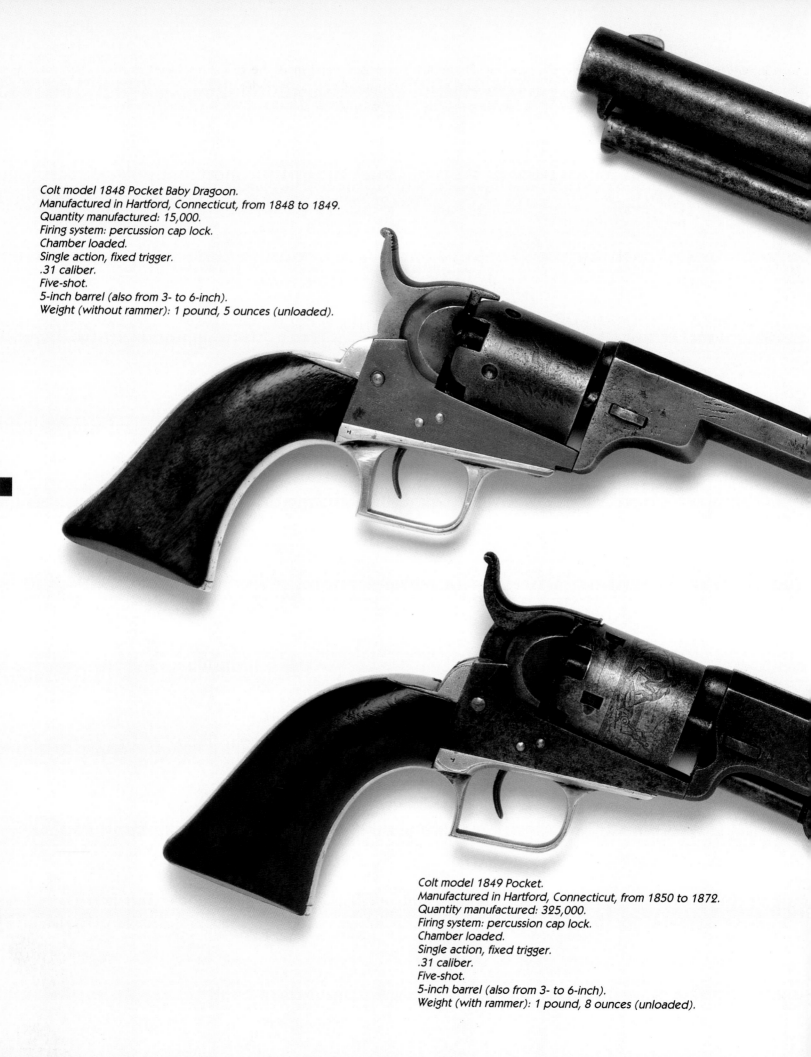

Colt model 1848 Pocket Baby Dragoon.
Manufactured in Hartford, Connecticut, from 1848 to 1849.
Quantity manufactured: 15,000.
Firing system: percussion cap lock.
Chamber loaded.
Single action, fixed trigger.
.31 caliber.
Five-shot.
5-inch barrel (also from 3- to 6-inch).
Weight (without rammer): 1 pound, 5 ounces (unloaded).

24

Colt model 1849 Pocket.
Manufactured in Hartford, Connecticut, from 1850 to 1872.
Quantity manufactured: 325,000.
Firing system: percussion cap lock.
Chamber loaded.
Single action, fixed trigger.
.31 caliber.
Five-shot.
5-inch barrel (also from 3- to 6-inch).
Weight (with rammer): 1 pound, 8 ounces (unloaded).

Shown here are three revolvers from the Colt Dragoon family. The Colt Baby Dragoon is a pocket revolver for use in the city. The trigger guard is square-backed and the cylinder's locking notches are oval like those of the big Dragoon No.1. It was manufactured both with and without the rammer. In the latter case there is no opening in the console and the cylinder axis pin is used after breaking open to eject the bullets. This model version is the rarest and the most coveted by collectors. The cylinder carries an engraving showing a battle with Indians or a stagecoach attack.

The Colt model 1849 Pocket was manufactured between 1850 and 1872. It differs from the previous model by its rounded trigger guard and rectangular cylinder notches. This model anticipated the Colt model 1851 Navy. Manufactured with several different barrel lengths (both with and without rammer), it was a great success, as the production numbers of 325,000 show.

Colt model 1851 Army Dragoon No. 3. Manufactured in Hartford, Connecticut, from 1851 to 1861. Quantity manufactured: 9,500. Firing system: percussion cap lock. Chamber loaded. Single action, fixed trigger. .44 caliber. Six-shot. 7 1/2-inch barrel. Weight: 4 pounds, 2 ounces (unloaded).

It may look like a strange insect, but in fact it is a dismantled Wesson & Leavitt revolver shown here. It has several special mechanical features and indirectly played an important role in the history of Colt revolvers. This .28- or .31-caliber pocket revolver is based on the Leavitt patent granted on April 29, 1837. The barrel tips upwards to disengage the cylinder and facilitate loading. The cylinder axis pin is used like a reloading rod. This model uses a Maynard primer (patented in 1845) which functions a little like the ribbon in a child's cap gun. There are no chimneys at the back of the cylinder to house metallic caps. The Wesson brothers (later of Smith & Wesson) manufactured the first military model. In June 1851, in a Boston courtroom, Samuel Colt successfully sued the Massachusetts Arms Company for patent infringement, and maintained a virtual monopoly on revolver manufacturing across the United States until his patent expired in 1857.

After 1857, Wesson & Leavitt were able to resume operations, but not for long. This time the Wesson brothers had learned better. When Daniel B. Wesson, shareholder in the Massachusetts Arms Company, founded his own manufacturing company with Horace Smith, he obtained a patent on his metal-case cartridge revolver and established his own monopoly.

Wesson & Leavitt Pocket.
Manufactured by Massachusetts Arms Company from 1851 to 1860.
Quantity manufactured: 3,000.
Firing system: Maynard cap ribbon.
Chamber loaded.
Single action, fixed trigger.
.31 caliber (.28 caliber also made).
Six-shot.
3 ½-inch or 2 ½-inch barrel.

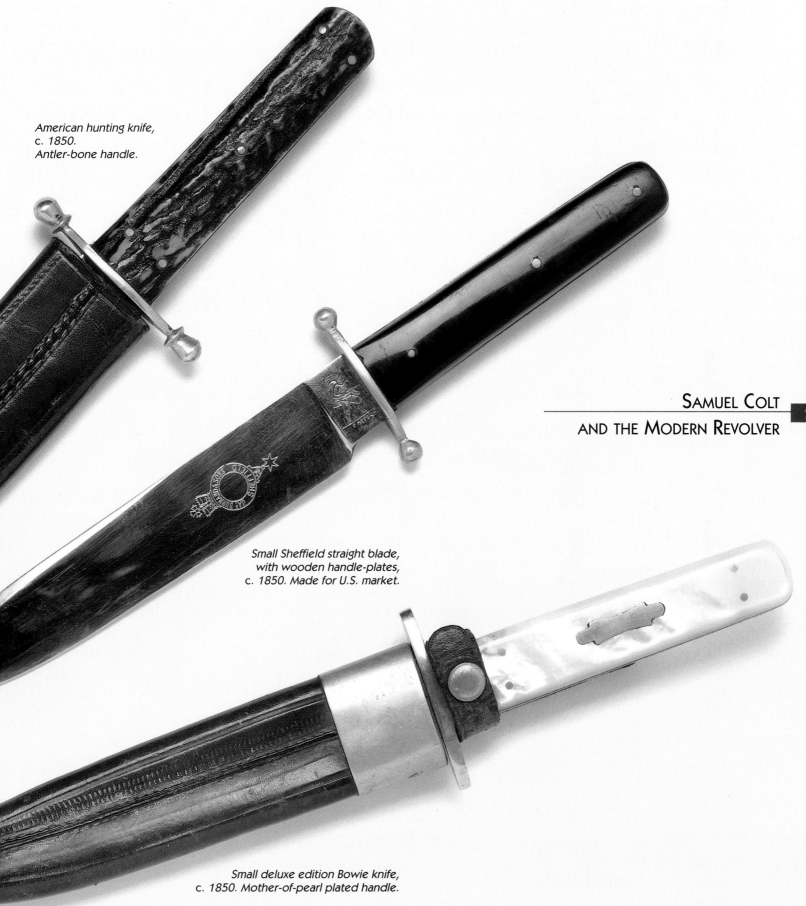

American hunting knife,
c. 1850.
Antler-bone handle.

Small Sheffield straight blade,
with wooden handle-plates,
c. 1850. Made for U.S. market.

Small deluxe edition Bowie knife,
c. 1850. Mother-of-pearl plated handle.

Main Street of Guthrie, Oklahoma. The photograph was taken just after a Doolin Gang raid. The men at the doorstep holding rifles helped track down the bandits. The towns of the West during their constructions all looked like this—dusty streets lined with clapboard storefronts. Some of these towns sprang up and disappeared overnight, slapped together in a few weeks, then shut down when their inhabitants moved on. Such was the case for gold-rush towns in California, Alaska, and Colorado, but also for big cattle-towns like Abilene, Kansas, which flourished for five years, from 1867 to 1872. In 1867, 35,000 heads of cattle arrived from Texas. Two years later, the figure was ten times higher. Served by the railroad, which linked it to the industrial towns of the Northeast, Abilene was the principal cattle-town west of the Mississippi. Huge herds of Texan cattle were convoyed here during the three-month cattle-run season, driven from watering hole to watering hole along the trails by gun-toting cowboys—usually Confederate veterans. During the summer months the town of Abilene became one of the most animated spots on earth, with hundreds of cattle changing hands and being shipped off north in the cattle cars of the Kansas Pacific Railroad. Wagon-team drivers, cowboys, salesmen, speculators, workers, bandits, and beasts filled the streets, and the sounds of horses and cattle filled the air, along with the crack of whips and the report of revolvers.

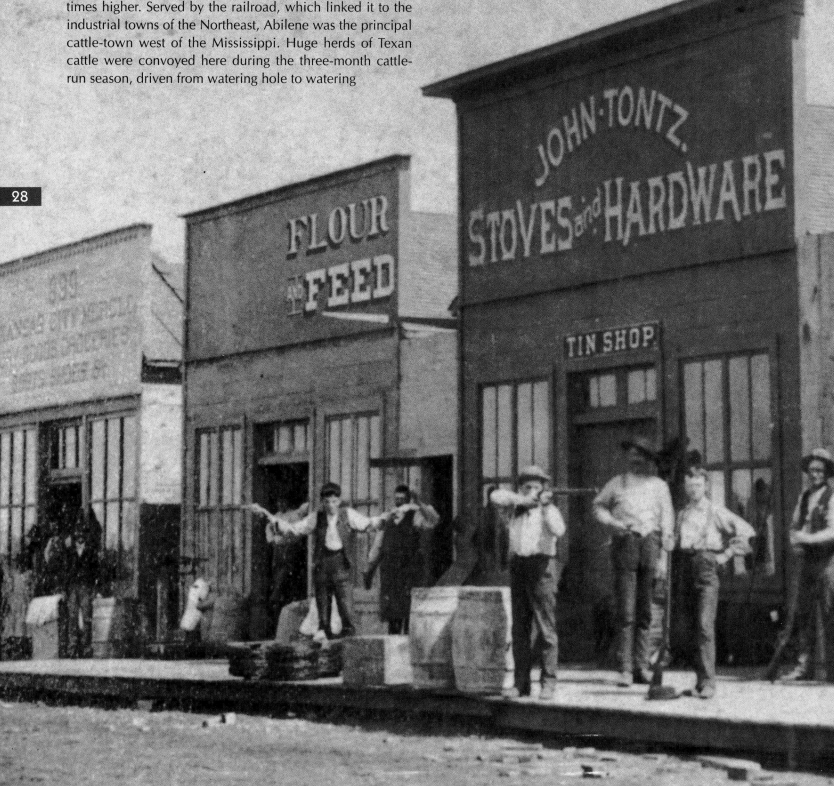

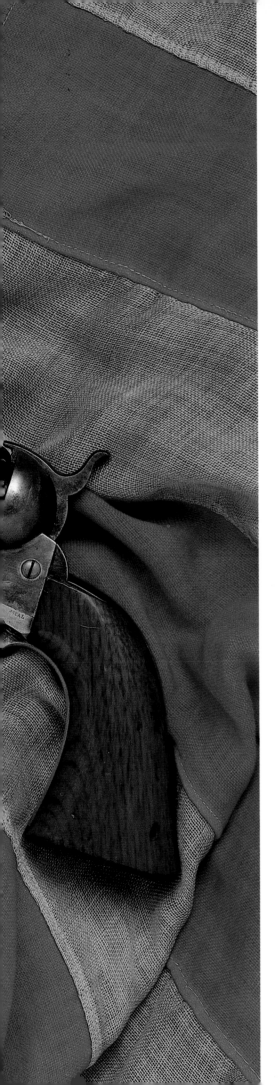

THE CIVIL WAR (1861-1865)

In the early dawn light of April 12, 1861, the first shell exploded in the Civil War between the Confederate States of the South and the Union of the North. Both sides thought it would be a short war, but it was to last four long years and remains the bloodiest conflict in America's history. A third more casualties were sustained by Americans than in the Second World War (618,000 as opposed to 407,000) and by a population seven times smaller. In 1861 the States were not united. America was not one but two distinct and hostile nations: North and South. Everything seemed different about them: population, traditions, culture, climate, economy, and, of course, the slavery issue. The industrial North, with four times the population, had a crushing material advantage; the South, aristocratic and rural, had almost no industry and was strangled by the naval blockade off its coasts. But it was willing to fight for its survival, and it had the best military leaders.

The revolver played an important role in the war. It was the cavalry's weapon of choice, and each man generally carried two of them. It was also the preferred weapon of the officers. It is estimated that 750,000 revolvers of all makes were bought by the North's armies and militias from 1861 to 1865. The Colt Company alone sold 386,417 revolvers during the war. Remington sold 133,029 revolvers of different models to the North's government. The South, on the other hand, had great difficulty arming itself. It bought Colt and Starr on the black market and Perrin, Lefaucheux, and Le Mat revolvers from Europe. It tried making its own guns locally but managed to produce only about 20,000 slipshod, poor-quality firearms in all. In the end the Confederates were forced to rely on the spoils of war, and, finally, 250,000 revolvers were brought across their borders.

On the Union flag, two .44 Colt model 1860 Army revolvers, including a deluxe model with ivory grip.

Colt model 1851 Navy revolver.
Manufactured in Hartford, Connecticut, from 1851 to 1872 (215,348).
Manufactured in London, England, from 1853 to 1856 (42,000).
Firing system: percussion cap lock.
Chamber loaded.
Single action, fixed trigger.
.36 caliber.
Six-shot.
Engraving on cylinder represents the naval battle of May 16, 1843.
7 $\frac{1}{2}$-inch octagonal barrel.
Weight: 2 pounds, 10 ounces (unloaded).

Engraved model manufactured in London, England.

Original engraved model manufactured in Hartford, Connecticut.

Engraved model manufactured in Hartford, Connecticut, marked "New York City."

Ten years before the Civil War broke out, Samuel Colt caused a great sensation when he presented his revolvers, notably his brand new model, the Navy, at the Great Exhibition of 1851 in London, England. An improved .36-caliber version of the Baby Dragoon, the Navy was light, elegant, and packed considerable firepower. The young industrialist saw that after conquering America, the European market was his for the taking. On New Year's Day, 1853, he opened a factory in London to manufacture the Navy model. Between 1853 and 1854, Colt toured the capitals of Europe, going as far afield as Constantinople in the hope of securing military contracts for his guns. By playing enemies off each other, using bribes and leaking information about possible or impending contracts with hostile powers, Colt was able to obtain orders from the Turks, who despised the Russians, and from the English, who were worried about the Russian encroachment on the Bosphorus. When the Crimean War broke out in 1854, Russian, English, and Turkish troops carried Colts. The Russian Colts were manufactured under subcontract in Belgium. In this period, Colt took on his new continental competitors, most notably the Adams revolvers. Sensing which way the wind was blowing, he realized that the end of the Crimean War would mean the end of his military contracts and so closed his London factory in 1856. The 1851 Navy continued to be produced in Hartford and was used throughout the American Civil War.

General Robert E. Lee on his horse, Traveller. Commander-in-Chief of the Virginia army in 1862, and leader of the Confederate armies in 1865, opposed to secession, he was adored by his soldiers and feared and admired by his enemies. He took up arms to defend his home, Virginia, when it was threatened by Northern advances. A savior, sometimes compared with Napoleon, he is considered one of America's greatest military strategists. He was, nonetheless, beaten at the Battle of Gettysburg. Of the 160,000 soldiers on both sides, more than 40,000 died during the three-day battle at the beginning of July 1863, in Pennsylvania, which the Southerners had reached with rare audacity. At two critical moments of the battle, held back by the equivocation of two subordinates, General Lee was obliged to undertake a difficult retreat to Virginia. After two years of desperate combat, General Lee was worn out by the fighting and by the misdeeds of Grant's assistant, the ferocious General Sherman, the real "executioner" of the South and particularly of Georgia, which he had promised would "scream with pain." Crushed by the superiority of its enemies, starving and completely worn out by four years of war, the South was forced to capitulate. On April 9, 1865, Lee agreed to meet Grant at Appotomax. At three o'clock, sitting opposite his enemies, he respectfully signed the South's surrender. In tears, the Southerners handed over their arms, but kept their horses, which they would need for the next harvest—the only generous gesture by their victor. General Lee's personal revolver, a Colt Root 1855, is kept in the Confederate Museum in Richmond, Virginia.

In 1860, with the army behind him, Sam Colt brought out a new military model destined to replace the Dragoon: the 1860 Army. It keeps the same powerful .44 caliber but is less cumbersome than the Dragoon, lighter, and more elegant. The grip is notched to receive a removable shoulder stock. The rammer lever has been modified and is now rack-driven. The frame and the rammer are marbled. The grip base is made of brass, the barrel and cylinder of blackened bronze. The grip is either wood or ivory. A small number (4,000) of the early models of this gun have an un-reinforced cylinder. It became the preferred revolver of the cavalry in the Civil War, and stayed in service well after, especially in the holsters of the men on the frontier. Its open frame is slightly delicate in action. John Wesley Hardin, outlaw in spite of himself, wrote in his

memoirs, "My old Colt 1860 Army has fired so much that there is a gap of at least ¹⁄₁₆ inch between the cylinder and the barrel. For each shot, you have to press the cylinder against the barrel with your left hand to maintain the pressure."

A year after Sam Colt died the company brought out the .36-caliber 1862 Police. It was a very light and elegant revolver, a smaller version of the 1860 Army. One of the people to use the gun was William Quantrill, celebrated Confederate from Kansas.

Colt model 1862 Police.
Manufactured in Hartford, Connecticut, from 1861 to 1872 .
Quantity manufactured: 28,000.
Firing system: percussion cap lock.
Chamber loaded.
Single action, fixed trigger.
.36 caliber.
Five-shot grooved cylinder.
6 ½-inch round barrel (a 4 ½-inch version also exists).

Colt model 1860 Army.
Manufactured in Hartford, Connecticut, from 1860 to 1872.
Quantity manufactured: 200,500.
Firing system: percussion cap lock.
Chamber loaded.
Single action, fixed trigger.
.44 caliber.
Six-shot.
Reinforced cylinder (except on the first produced).
Round 8-inch or, rarely, 7 ¹/₂-inch barrel.
Weight: 2 pounds, 11 ounces.

Remington Model 1863 Army.
Manufactured in Illion, New York, from
1863 to 1875.
Quantity manufactured: 132,000.
Firing system: percussion cap lock.
Chamber loaded.
Single action, fixed trigger.
.44 caliber.
Six-shot.
Solid frame.
8-inch octagonal barrel.

Flask comme-
morating the Civil
War (1861-1865).

Union officer's belt buckle,
Civil War period (1861-1865).

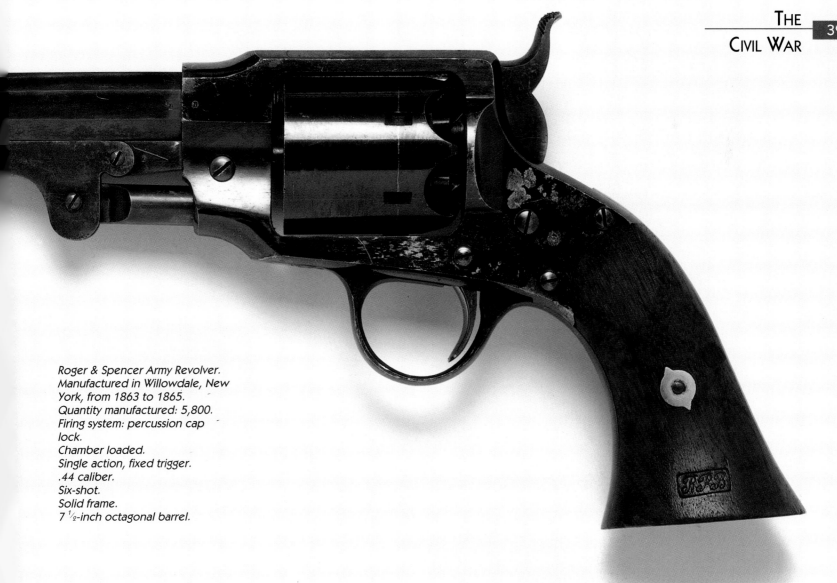

The huge demand for firearms during the Civil War went well beyond the production capacity of the Colt Company, the Union army's official supplier. The army had to turn to other manufacturers. The state militias, the units raised by private funds, and finally the individual soldiers themselves were buying up everything available. The Roger & Spencer revolver is a special case: 5,800 of them were manufactured for the Federal government between 1863 and 1865. Delivery came too late, though, as the war was already winding down. As a result, most of these revolvers never made it off the shelf, which explains their often excellent state of preservation.

The Remington revolvers are another story. They are part of a distinguished line of weapons created by Eliphalet Remington (1793-1861), a gun-barrel maker by trade. Starting out on his own in 1828, he invested little by little in machinery. By 1845 he had begun to win contracts with the army to produce rifled barrels for their guns. He brought his sons into the business and secured the services of certain inventors, notably Fordyce Beals, who created the first Remington revolver, a pocket model, in 1857. The next year, Beals finished work on a powerful military revolver, the 1858 Remington-Beals Army and Navy, which went into production in 1860 (2,500 were made for the army and 15,000 for the navy). It was superior to its competitors by virtue of the sturdiness of its solid-frame construction. The subsequent models, 1861 (10,000 for the army and 8,000 for the navy), and 1863 (132,000 for the army and 22,000 for the navy), were little more than variations on this original model.

Roger & Spencer Army Revolver. Manufactured in Willowdale, New York, from 1863 to 1865. Quantity manufactured: 5,800. Firing system: percussion cap lock. Chamber loaded. Single action, fixed trigger. .44 caliber. Six-shot. Solid frame. 7 ¹/₂-inch octagonal barrel.

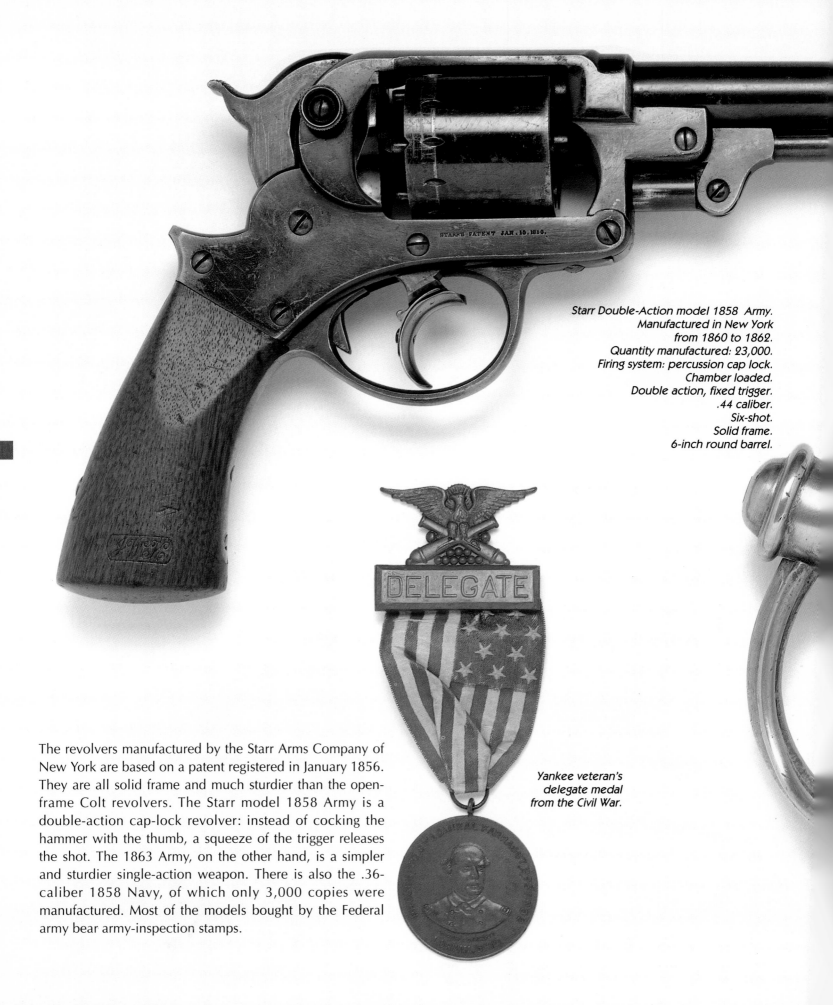

Starr Double-Action model 1858 Army.
Manufactured in New York
from 1860 to 1862.
Quantity manufactured: 23,000.
Firing system: percussion cap lock.
Chamber loaded.
Double action, fixed trigger.
.44 caliber.
Six-shot.
Solid frame.
6-inch round barrel.

Yankee veteran's
delegate medal
from the Civil War.

The revolvers manufactured by the Starr Arms Company of New York are based on a patent registered in January 1856. They are all solid frame and much sturdier than the open-frame Colt revolvers. The Starr model 1858 Army is a double-action cap-lock revolver: instead of cocking the hammer with the thumb, a squeeze of the trigger releases the shot. The 1863 Army, on the other hand, is a simpler and sturdier single-action weapon. There is also the .36-caliber 1858 Navy, of which only 3,000 copies were manufactured. Most of the models bought by the Federal army bear army-inspection stamps.

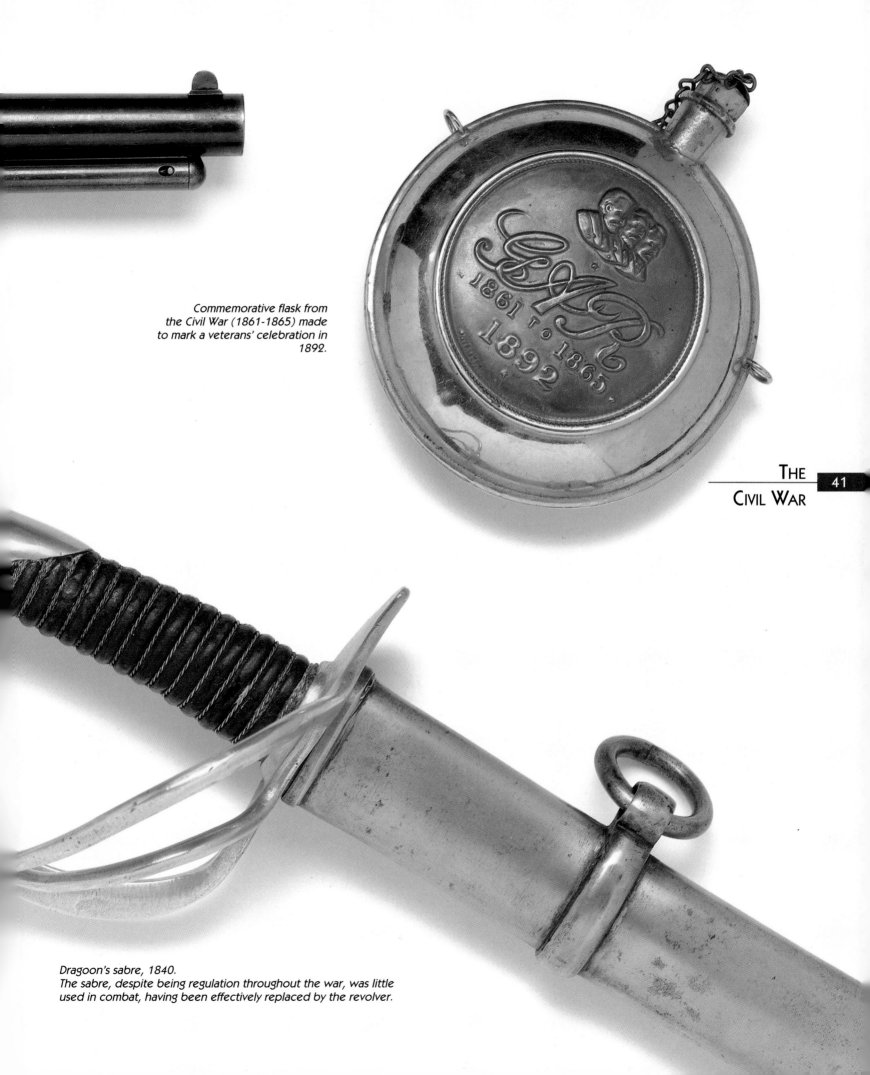

Commemorative flask from
the Civil War (1861-1865) made
to mark a veterans' celebration in
1892.

Dragoon's sabre, 1840.
The sabre, despite being regulation throughout the war, was little
used in combat, having been effectively replaced by the revolver.

Full charge
of a cavalry
officer of the
Confederate armies.
The holster contains a
rare and dangerous Le
Mat model, of which only
3,500 were made in New
Orleans, England, and France. The
standard-bearer brandishes the
second model of the Southern national
flag which replaces the "Stars and Bars,"
too often confused with the Union flag, the
"Stars and Stripes." The number of stars increased
from seven to thirteen as new members subscribed.
The thirteenth star represents part of the Indian nation
which joined the South.

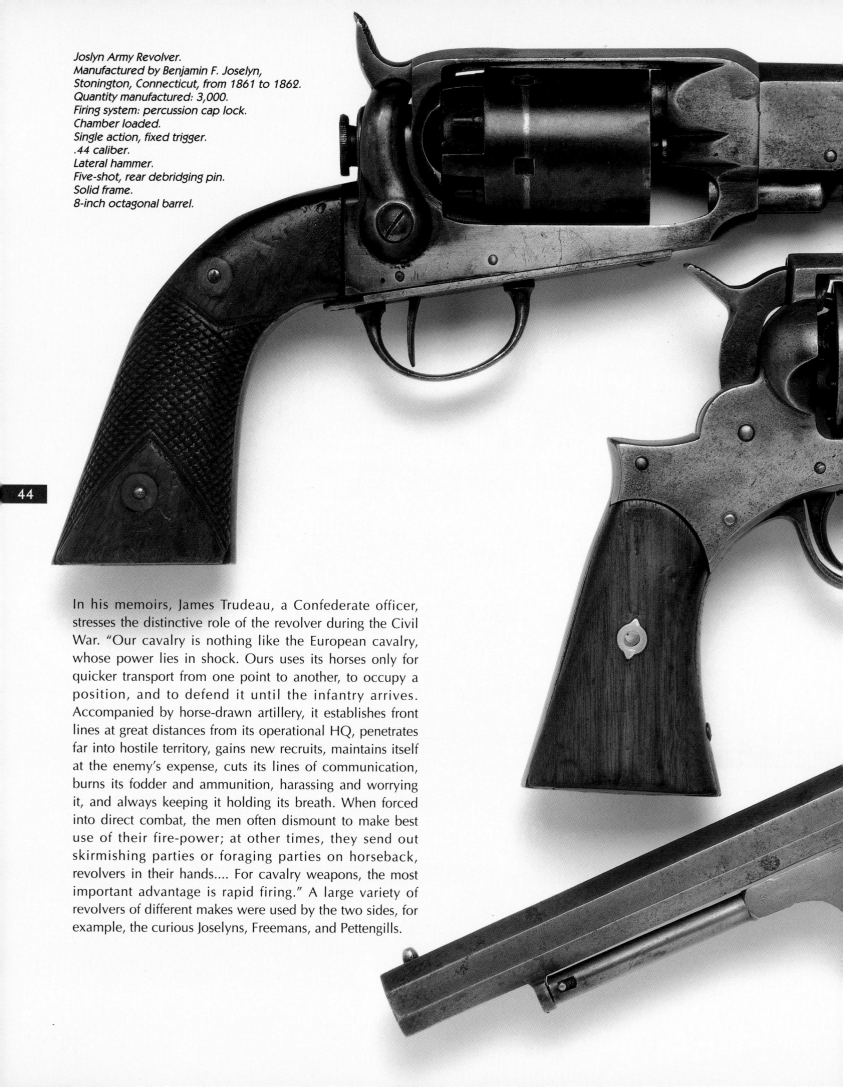

Joslyn Army Revolver.
Manufactured by Benjamin F. Joselyn,
Stonington, Connecticut, from 1861 to 1862.
Quantity manufactured: 3,000.
Firing system: percussion cap lock.
Chamber loaded.
Single action, fixed trigger.
.44 caliber.
Lateral hammer.
Five-shot, rear debridging pin.
Solid frame.
8-inch octagonal barrel.

44

In his memoirs, James Trudeau, a Confederate officer, stresses the distinctive role of the revolver during the Civil War. "Our cavalry is nothing like the European cavalry, whose power lies in shock. Ours uses its horses only for quicker transport from one point to another, to occupy a position, and to defend it until the infantry arrives. Accompanied by horse-drawn artillery, it establishes front lines at great distances from its operational HQ, penetrates far into hostile territory, gains new recruits, maintains itself at the enemy's expense, cuts its lines of communication, burns its fodder and ammunition, harassing and worrying it, and always keeping it holding its breath. When forced into direct combat, the men often dismount to make best use of their fire-power; at other times, they send out skirmishing parties or foraging parties on horseback, revolvers in their hands.... For cavalry weapons, the most important advantage is rapid firing." A large variety of revolvers of different makes were used by the two sides, for example, the curious Joselyns, Freemans, and Pettengills.

Austin T. Freeman Army Revolver.
Manufactured in New York from 1863 to 1864.
Quantity manufactured: 2,000.
Firing system: percussion cap lock.
Chamber loaded.
Single action, fixed trigger.
.44 caliber.
Six-shot.
Solid frame.
7 ½-inch round barrel.

Pettengill Army Revolver.
Manufactured by C.S. Pettengill, New Haven,
Connecticut, from 1861 to 1862 .
Quantity manufactured: 3,400.
Firing system: percussion cap lock.
Chamber loaded.
Double action, with no hammer.
.44 caliber.
Six-shot.
Solid frame.
7 ½-inch round barrel.

Figured on the Confederate flag alongside a Bowie knife, the Le Mat is the most renowned of the Yankee revolvers. Despite its popularity, only a limited number were actually delivered to Confederate forces (1,200 to the army and 600 to the marines). It fires ten consecutive rounds.

Its outstanding feature is its two barrels: one conventionally rifled .42 caliber serving the nine-shot cylinder, and the other, centered on the cylinder's axis, made for firing buckshot. The two barrels are fired by a single hammer which pivots from one chamber to the other. Those sold to the Confederates were all cap-lock muzzle-loaded models. The inventor of this singular weapon was the French doctor Jean-Alexandre-François Le Mat. Born in 1820, he emigrated to New Orleans after finishing his medical studies and was befriended by Pierre Toutant Beauregard, a future Confederate general.

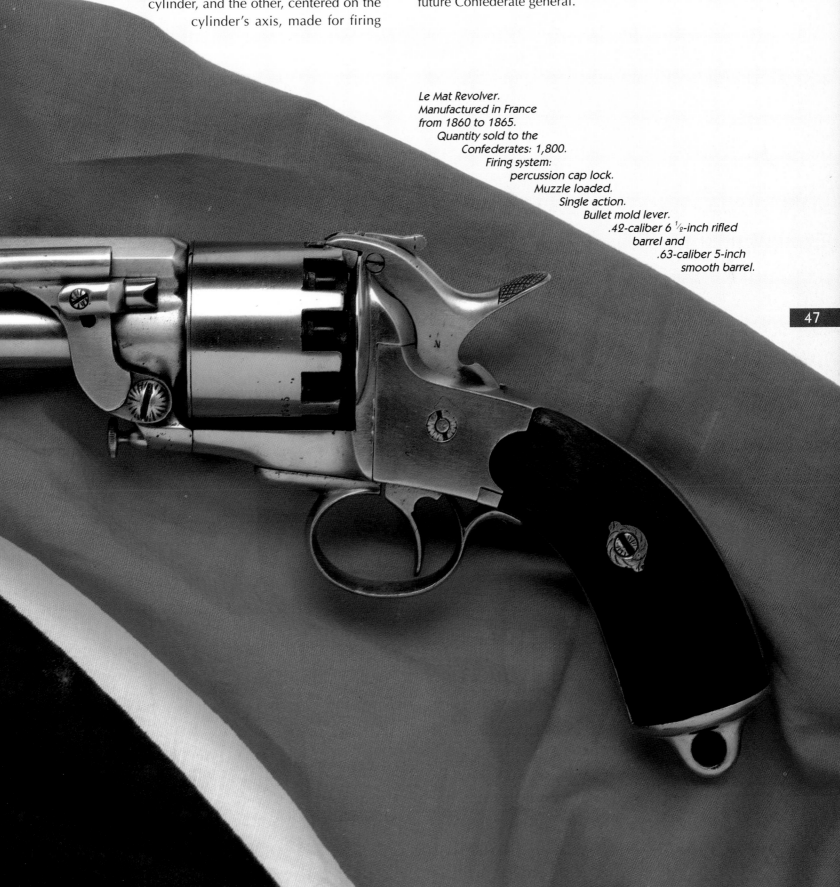

Le Mat Revolver.
Manufactured in France
from 1860 to 1865.
Quantity sold to the
Confederates: 1,800.
Firing system:
percussion cap lock.
Muzzle loaded.
Single action.
Bullet mold lever.
.42-caliber 6 ½-inch rifled
barrel and
.63-caliber 5-inch
smooth barrel.

BOXED AND ENGRAVED ARMS

Men have always had a special appreciation for deluxe and personalized firearms. Weapons showrooms and museums bear ample witness to the lavish decoration of old pistols and flintlock harquebuses ordered over the centuries by the famous and powerful from the greatest gunsmiths of their time. Beautiful arms were presented as gifts by princes and heads of state to forge and reinforce strategic links and friendships. This practice is relatively recent in American history but was quickly perfected by Samuel Colt in the nineteenth century. From his very beginnings in the trade, Colt understood the utility of offering a boxed set or engraved pistol as a way to get orders. Of the 42,000 1851 Navy revolvers manufactured between 1853 and 1856 at his factory in London, he gave away 89, in pairs or individually, to 62 different public figures in England alone. A quick look at the list shows that Colt aimed high, targetting such people as Prince Albert, husband of Queen Victoria; the Prince of Wales, next-in-line to the throne; the Duke of Wellington, War Minister; the Marquis of Anglesy, Master General of Supplies; and Lord Palmerston, the Prime Minister, to name but a few.

The list also included eleven newspaper publishers and eight ambassadors of foreign powers, such as Marshall Pélisier, France's ambassador to London. Napoleon III himself received an oak box containing a superb pair of Navy revolvers engraved with his monogram. The gift was no doubt appreciated, but, unfortunately for Colt, no orders were forthcoming from the French.

Colt box with deluxe .36-caliber 1851 Navy. Original ivory grip. The frame, barrel neck, hammer, and grip fittings are all hand engraved. The cylinder engraving appears on all 1851 Navy models. It depicts a naval battle fought by Commander Moore of the Texas marines against a superior Mexican fleet and bears the inscription "Engaged May 16, 1843." Moore was a staunch supporter of Colt revolvers.

In keeping with the European tradition of boxed sets of duelling and target-pistols, Colt produced, very early on in his career, beautiful cases to hold one or two revolvers. The weapons were always selected with great care, whether or not they were specially engraved. Here we see a case with a Colt model 1849 Dragoon No. 2. All the accessories are intact: a large powder horn, bullet mold, several bullets, and a primer tin. The weapon has almost never been fired and is in near-mint condition.

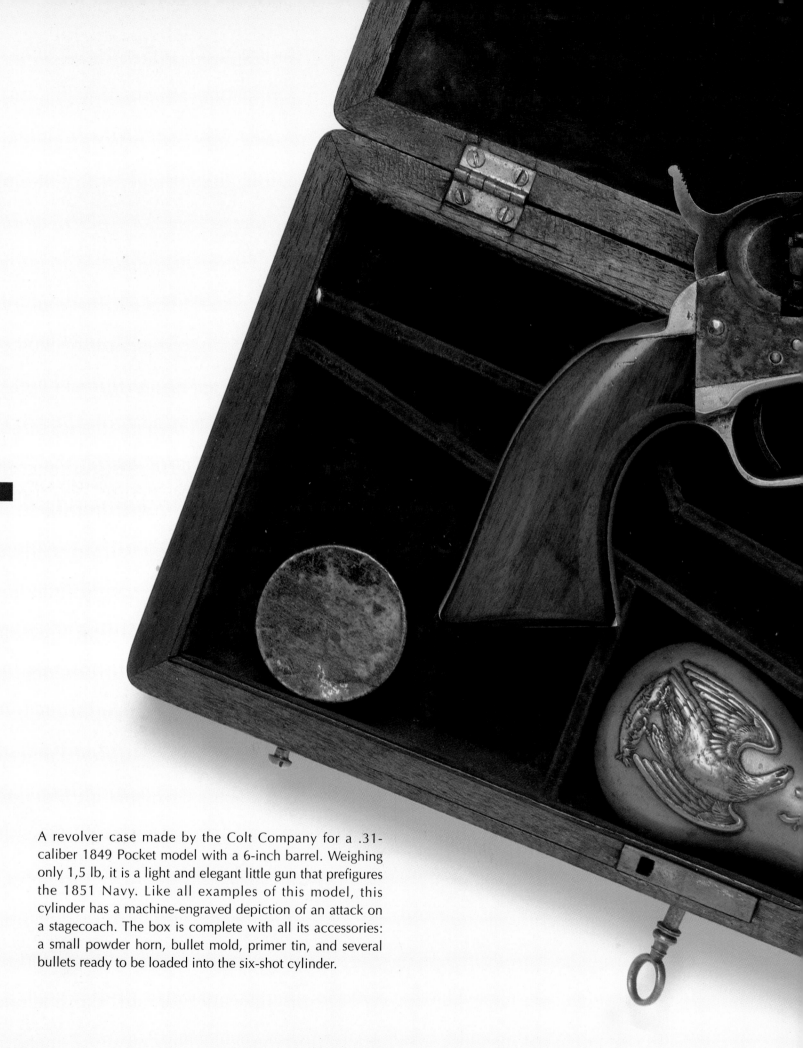

A revolver case made by the Colt Company for a .31-caliber 1849 Pocket model with a 6-inch barrel. Weighing only 1,5 lb, it is a light and elegant little gun that prefigures the 1851 Navy. Like all examples of this model, this cylinder has a machine-engraved depiction of an attack on a stagecoach. The box is complete with all its accessories: a small powder horn, bullet mold, primer tin, and several bullets ready to be loaded into the six-shot cylinder.

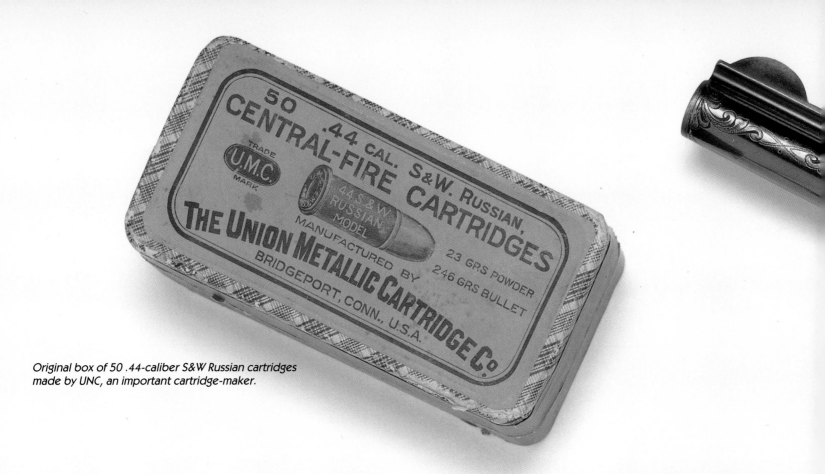

Original box of 50 .44-caliber S&W Russian cartridges
made by UNC, an important cartridge-maker.

Cleaning accessories.
Original ivory-handled cleaning rod
with two barrel brushes.

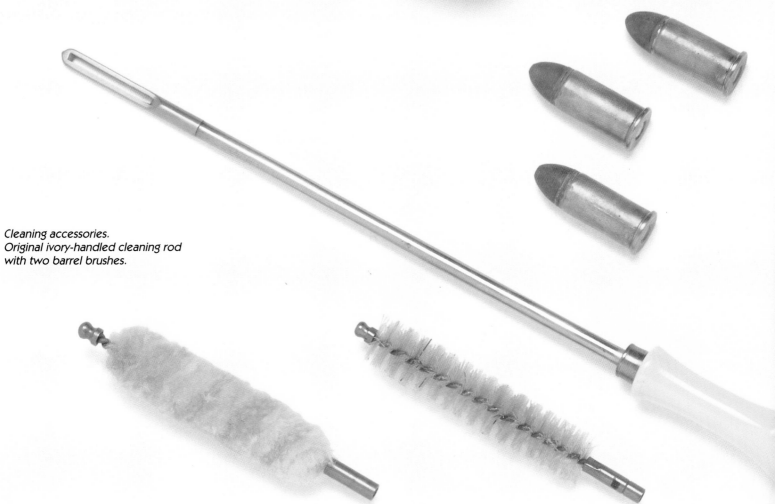

Smith & Wesson Russian Third Model (1874). Deluxe model factory-engraved by L.D. Nimschke, the foremost of S&W's engravers at that time. The crossed cannon barrels carved in deep relief on the ivory grip plates indicate that this weapon was likely made for an artillery officer. The accessories, including the ivory-handled cleaning rod and the .44-caliber Russian cartridges, are original.

"Home Sweet Home"
Colonel and Mrs. George Armstrong Custer at home in their parlor at Fort Lincoln, Dakota, in 1873. A great gun lover, Custer collected revolvers given to him by admirers. He remains one of the most controversial figures of the Old West. Romantic hero to some, ambitious egomaniac, or even a butcher, to others, he earned his provisional General's stars during the Civil War by virtue of his bravery on the battlefield, but also because of his brutality towards the Confederate populace.

Demoted at the end of the war like many others, he was a Lieutenant Colonel when the Indian Wars swept across the Plains. His murderous raid on a Cheyenne village on the banks of the Washita River on January 27, 1868, earned him a reputation as an Indian-killer, which was a mark of distinction in the high society of the East Coast at the time. The Cheyenne Indians and others exacted their revenge on the morning of June 25, 1876, at Little Big Horn. Hoping to carry off what he thought would be an easy raid, Custer, along with three companies of the 7th Cavalry, rode blindly into a trap that morning. Surrounded by a horde of Sioux, Cheyenne, and Crow warriors, Custer and all of his 230 men were killed. It was the worst disaster ever to befall the U.S. army. That day, Custer was armed with a pair of Webley RIC .450-caliber revolvers, given to him by Lord Berkeley in 1869 in thanks for an excellent hunting expedition. The revolvers have never been recovered.

Gun case commemorating the "Sesquicentennial Samuel Colt 1814-1964." Made by the Colt Company in 1964 to celebrate the one hundred and fiftieth birthday of the founder, this box contains a Colt model 1873 Single-Action Army (Cavalry Model) with a 7-inch barrel. It has a special finish and silver-plated and engraved cylinder and fittings. It is accompanied by twelve car-

tridges and a silver medallion made for this occasion. Specially numbered editions of the deluxe-finish commemorative arms, such as those of the Colt Company, among others, are eagerly sought by collectors, and increase steadily in value over time.

In a leather travel case bearing the name of William & Powell, a well-known Liverpool armory, is a beautiful Smith & Wesson No. 3 New Model Target. It is a professional competition issue of the New Model No. 3, which was manufactured between 1878 and 1919, with a total production of 35,796. Like all the Smith & Wesson No. 3s, the New Model is based on a patent registered on August 24, 1869. The first 13,000 manufactured were single action with a recoiling hammer and rack-and-gear extractor, patented in February 20, 1877, after which it was equipped with a bolt extractor (patented in May 11, 1880). The New Model is identifiable by its extremely short extractor housing below the barrel.

Boxes containing contemporary revolvers by two competitors. The top one is a superb little center-fire Colt model 1877 Double-Action. It is a deluxe nickel-plated edition with ivory grip. The Colt Company gave two different names to this model, according to its caliber. The .38 is called the Lightning; the .41 the Thunderer. Between the two of them, 166,849 copies of the Colt 1877 Double-Action were manufactured between 1877 and 1909.

The other box, quite rare, contains a .32-caliber Merwin Hulbert Double-Action Pocket with two barrels of different lengths. These revolvers were manufactured by Hopkins & Allen of Norwich, Connecticut. The upper

rib of the barrel is stamped with patent notices 1877, 1880, 1882, and 1883. While it is not known how many of this model were manufactured, the number could not have exceeded a few thousand.

62

Smith & Wesson .38 Baby Russian Second Model.
Break-open barrel with rod extractor (simultaneous extractor).
.38 caliber.
Completely engraved deluxe version, with mother-of-pearl grip plates.

Smith & Wesson No. 1½ Second Issue.
.32-caliber rimfire.
Engraved version with mother-of-pearl plates.

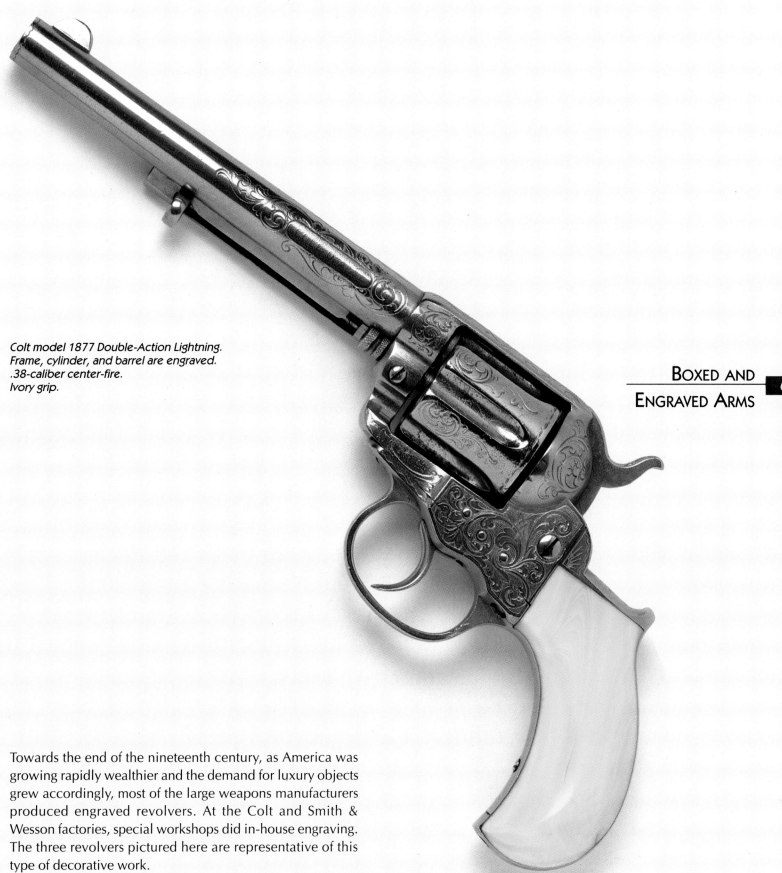

Colt model 1877 Double-Action Lightning.
Frame, cylinder, and barrel are engraved.
.38-caliber center-fire.
Ivory grip.

Towards the end of the nineteenth century, as America was
growing rapidly wealthier and the demand for luxury objects
grew accordingly, most of the large weapons manufacturers
produced engraved revolvers. At the Colt and Smith &
Wesson factories, special workshops did in-house engraving.
The three revolvers pictured here are representative of this
type of decorative work.

Attractive red velvet-lined box containing a bronze Smith & Wesson .44 Double-Action. The Double-Action revolver allows firing without manually cocking the hammer. Squeezing the trigger automatically cocks the hammer and rotates the cylinder (first action), then releases the hammer onto the cartridge (second action). The first Smith & Wesson Double-Action mechanism was patented on October 16, 1879, by J.H. Ballard. Production began in 1880 with a .38 caliber with a simultaneous break-open extractor of the New Model type. This firearm has exceptional balance in the hand.

SMITH & WESSON

Working in the Robbins & Lawrence cannon factory in Windsor, Vermont, were two gunsmiths, Horace Smith (1808-1893) and Daniel B. Wesson (1825-1906). Their two names appeared together for the first time on February 14, 1854, on a patent for a repeating revolver: the Volcanic. On June 20, 1854, the Smith & Wesson Company was founded and began production of this pistol. It was a financial disaster, however, and the two inventors ended up selling off the patents and their machinery. But they had other plans in mind and were already working towards the release of a truly "revolutionary" revolver in 1857, the year the great Sam Colt's legal monopoly was due to expire. In August of 1854 they registered a patent on a small metal-case cartridge inspired by the work of the Frenchman Flobert. It was the birth of the modern rimfire cartridge. It would be made in all calibers, from .22 to .44, but was to have its first incarnation in their future revolver. In 1856, Smith & Wesson bought a patent—one that Colt had overlooked, owned by one Rollin White—that gave them exclusive rights until 1869 to manufacture metal-case cartridge, chamber-loaded revolvers.

Their first small pocket pistol, the No.1, was ready in 1857. The number designates the frame of the weapon, thus the No.1 is a sturdier model, followed by the No.2 in 1861 and the No.3 in 1869. The No.3 was the first truly satisfactory simultaneous extractor revolver to be made. Their first double-action revolver came out in 1880, the first swinging cylinder, the .32-caliber Hand Ejector, in 1896, and then in 1905, the illustrious Military & Police, whose mechanism is used to this day in Smith & Wesson revolvers.

Smith & Wesson No. 3 New Model, manufactured from 1878 on the same patent used by all No. 3s, but improved by a patent of February 20, 1877, with a modified extractor. Another such modification was introduced in 1880 with the bolt extractor replacing the rack extractor. This was the type of revolver used to gun down Jesse James on April 3, 1882.

It all began in 1846 when Walter Hunt, inventor of the safety pin, the fountain pen, and other such contemporary wonders, registered patents for a self-propelled projectile with the charge contained in a hollow bullet, and a repeating gun theoretically capable of firing this bullet. In need of money, Hunt sold the patent to the gunsmith Lewis Jennings, who made several improvements on it, and registered them in 1849. The package of patents was then sold again and ended up in Horace Smith's hands, who in turn improved upon the ensemble. In 1851 he patented a repeating pistol with a tubular magazine beneath the barrel. The repeating mechanism is activated by a safety lever, exactly like on the future Winchester carbines, and with good reason, as we shall see.

On June 20, 1854, Smith and Wesson founded their company, setting out initially to manufacture the pistol that was to become known to collectors as the Volcanic. This pistol used bullets containing their own charges and caps but was not without its shortcomings. Business was bad. A year later, the two inventors sold off the patent and machinery to the Volcanic Repeating Arms Company, one of whose associates was the shirt-maker Oliver Winchester. Acting on his own, Winchester bought the S&W patent and machines for a pittance and, with the help of an excellent engineer, Benjamin Tyler Henry, began working on the carbine that would bear his name. But that is another story . . .

The Volcanic repeating pistols fall into three groups according to their manufacture. A first run was made by Smith & Wesson from 1854-1855 in Norwich, Connecticut. They produced a total of 1,600 round-butt .31-caliber No.1s and square-butt .41-caliber No.2s. After the sale to Volcanic in New Haven, roughly three thousand .38 calibers were made between 1855-1857. The real Volcanics can be distinguished from the Smith & Wessons by their uniformly octagonal barrels, their predecessors being octagonal only for the first third of the barrel and round for the rest. Production continued when the Volcanic was bought out in 1857 by the New Haven Arms Company (which was soon to be controlled by Oliver Winchester), with a total of 3,200 pistols being made up to the year 1860.

Volcanic repeating pistols.
Patented by Smith & Wesson in 1851.
Manufactured by the Volcanic Repeating Arms Company, New Haven, Connecticut, from 1855-1857.
Quantity manufactured: 3,000.
Firing system: self-propelling fulminate charge.
Manually repeating.
Tubular magazine beneath the barrel.
.38 caliber.
6-inch octagonal barrel (below); 8-inch octagonal barrel (above).

Smith & Wesson No.1 First Issue.
Manufactured in Springfield,
Massachusetts, from 1857 to 1860.
Quantity manufactured: 11,671.
Single action.
.22-caliber rimfire.
Seven-shot.
Squared butt.
Brass frame.
3 ³/₁₆ - inch octagonal ribbed barrel.
Small circular cover plate.

Smith & Wesson No.1 First Issue (6th type).
Like the model above, but with a steel frame.

Original Smith & Wesson box
for the little No.1 First Issue
revolvers.

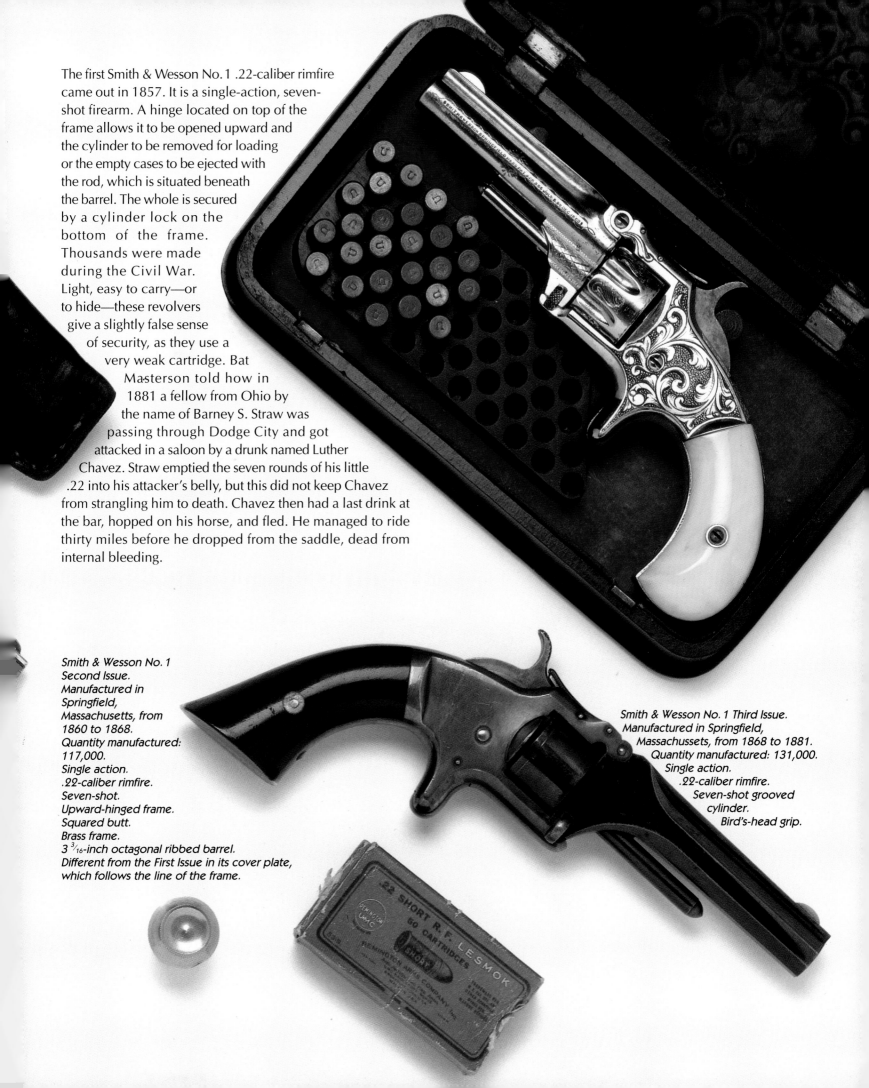

The first Smith & Wesson No. 1 .22-caliber rimfire came out in 1857. It is a single-action, seven-shot firearm. A hinge located on top of the frame allows it to be opened upward and the cylinder to be removed for loading or the empty cases to be ejected with the rod, which is situated beneath the barrel. The whole is secured by a cylinder lock on the bottom of the frame. Thousands were made during the Civil War. Light, easy to carry—or to hide—these revolvers give a slightly false sense of security, as they use a very weak cartridge. Bat Masterson told how in 1881 a fellow from Ohio by the name of Barney S. Straw was passing through Dodge City and got attacked in a saloon by a drunk named Luther Chavez. Straw emptied the seven rounds of his little .22 into his attacker's belly, but this did not keep Chavez from strangling him to death. Chavez then had a last drink at the bar, hopped on his horse, and fled. He managed to ride thirty miles before he dropped from the saddle, dead from internal bleeding.

Smith & Wesson No. 1 Second Issue. Manufactured in Springfield, Massachusetts, from 1860 to 1868. Quantity manufactured: 117,000. Single action. .22-caliber rimfire. Seven-shot. Upward-hinged frame. Squared butt. Brass frame. 3 3/16-inch octagonal ribbed barrel. Different from the First Issue in its cover plate, which follows the line of the frame.

Smith & Wesson No. 1 Third Issue. Manufactured in Springfield, Massachussets, from 1868 to 1881. Quantity manufactured: 131,000. Single action. .22-caliber rimfire. Seven-shot grooved cylinder. Bird's-head grip.

Smith & Wesson No. 1½ (2nd type).
Manufactured from 1865 to 1868.
Quantity manufactured: 26,300.
Single action.
.32-caliber rimfire.
Five-shot.
Upward-hinged frame.
Bird's-head grip.
Steel frame.
4-inch round ribbed barrel
(3-inch version also exists).

Original oilcan.

Smith & Wesson
No. 1½ (2nd type).
Ivory grip.
Nickel frame.

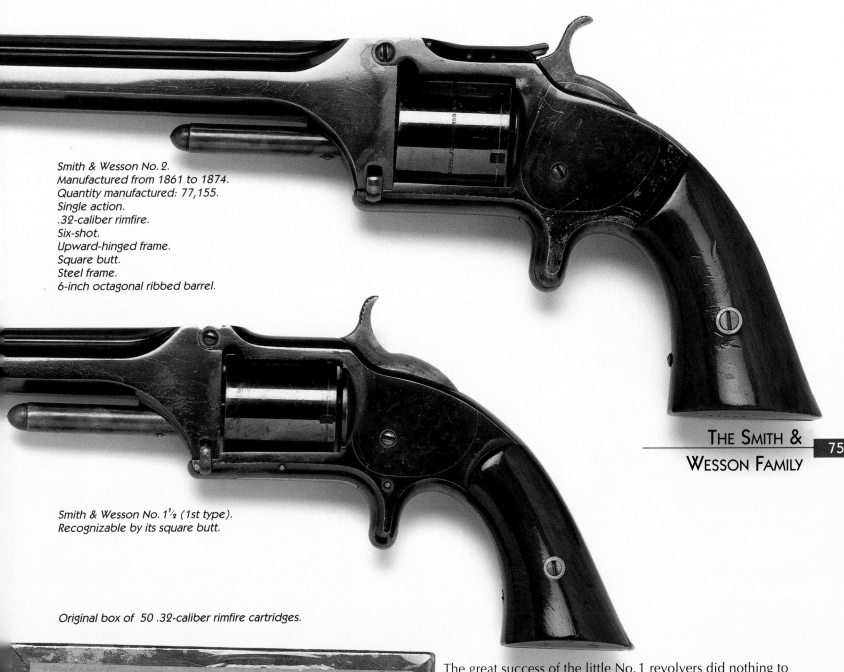

Smith & Wesson No. 2.
Manufactured from 1861 to 1874.
Quantity manufactured: 77,155.
Single action.
.32-caliber rimfire.
Six-shot.
Upward-hinged frame.
Square butt.
Steel frame.
6-inch octagonal ribbed barrel.

Smith & Wesson No. 1½ (1st type).
Recognizable by its square butt.

Original box of 50 .32-caliber rimfire cartridges.

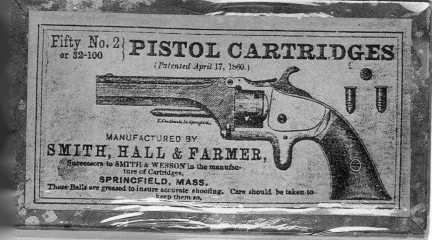

The great success of the little No. 1 revolvers did nothing to slow down Smith & Wesson. Now they were researching a more powerful model capable of interesting the military. They settled on a .32-caliber rimfire. The weapon, and the cartridge conceived for it, were called the No. 2. The new revolver has the same shape as the No. 1, but is much larger. It was introduced in 1861 at the beginning of the Civil War and was used by many well-known names from the Old West, including Jesse James, General Custer, and General Rutherford Hayes, the nineteenth president.

In 1865 the two partners designed a second .32-caliber rimfire, but this one was not as large as the No. 2: it was thus called the No. 1. Its shape and mechanics were identical to those of the No. 1 Second Issue, though the dimensions were different and the frame was made of steel.

In May 1870, Smith & Wesson began production of a large revolver that they had developed the year before, the No. 3 American Model. It was at first designed to fire the .44-caliber rimfire cartridge from Winchester's 1866 carbine. But S&W coveted the army's business, so to bring the weapon into line with their needs, they quickly replaced the rimfire with a center-fire, the Smith & Wesson 44/100.

*Smith & Wesson American
No. 3 First Model.
Manufactured from
1870 to 1872.
Quantity manufactured: 8,000.
Single action.
.44-caliber S&W center-fire.
Six-shot.
Downward-hinged frame.
Square butt.
Steel frame.
8-inch round ribbed barrel.*

This No. 3 Model, the first large-frame pattern, includes the exciting new feature of a simultaneous break-open extractor, patented in August 1869. It also has a steel frame, square grip, a cover plate fastened by three screws, auto-ejecting action, an anvil in front of the firing pin, and an oval steel trigger guard screwed to the frame. The star-shaped simultaneous extractor extends when the barrel is broken open, thanks to a rack mechanism. The barrel is locked to the frame with a T-bolt, which itself acts as the rear sight. Among the great names of the day to use the American No. 3 Model were Jesse James and "Texas Jack" Omohundra, cowboy, scout from the Indian Wars, and close friend of Buffalo Bill.

*Smith & Wesson American No. 3 Second Model.
Manufactured from 1872 to 1874.
Quantity manufactured: 20,735.
Single action.
.44-caliber S&W center-fire.
Six-shot.
Downward-hinged frame.
Square butt.
Steel frame.
8-inch round ribbed barrel.
Recognizable by the slight bulge in the frame
for the reinforced trigger pin.*

Smith & Wesson did not convince the army to adopt their big No. 3 revolver, but they did have better luck with the Russian army, which was undergoing a major reorganization at the time. The two industrialists managed to win over General Gorloff, Russia's military attaché in Washington, who, on May 1, 1871, signed a contract for a first order of 20,000 revolvers. Gorloff and his assistant, Captain Kasavery Ordinetz, insisted on a number of modifications to the American Model, the most important of which had to do with the cartridge itself, which was to have a heavier bullet, a slightly wider case, and a superior powder charge. Thus was born the .44 Russian, more powerful by far than the original .44 S&W. Aside from the cartridge, the Russians wanted cyrillic lettering on the barrel and a lanyard swivel on the butt. Afterwards they asked for more changes again, which allow us today to distinguish three different Russian Models. The First Model has a square butt with a lanyard ring. The Second Model was given a rounded butt with a lanyard ring and a trigger guard with finger-rest. On the Third Model, the hammer has a notch which grips the barrel-lock onto the barrel-catch. The extractor has a sort of clutch, and the extracting mechanism has been altered. The cylinder catch is fastened on by a large milled screw above the barrel.

Smith & Wesson Russian First Model.
Manufactured from 1870 to 1874.
Quantity manufactured: 5,165 commercially;
20,014 on contract to Russia.
Single action.
.44-caliber Russian.
Six-shot.
Downward-hinged frame.
Simultaneous break-open extractor.
8-inch round ribbed barrel.

Smith & Wesson Russian Second Model.
Manufactured from 1873 to 1878.
Quantity manufactured: 15,200 commercially;
70,000 on contract to Russia.
Single action.
.44-caliber Russian.
Six-shot.
Downward-hinged frame.
Simultaneous break-open extractor.
7-inch round ribbed barrel.

Smith & Wesson Russian Third Model.
Manufactured from 1874 to 1878.
Quantity manufactured: 60,638 commercially;
41,138 on contract to Russia.
Single action.
.44-caliber Russian.
Six-shot.
Downward-hinged frame.
Simultaneous break-open extractor.
6 ½-inch round ribbed barrel.

In the winter of 1871-1872, Grand Duke Alexis (in the center of the photograph), 22-year-old son of Czar Alexander II and brother of the future Alexander III, was officially welcomed to the U.S. by President Grant. On December 6, he travelled to Springfield to visit Smith & Wesson, who had only recently become official suppliers to the Russian army. They presented him with a specially engraved Russian Model. A special luxury train was put at his disposal for his visit. In Chicago he asked General Sheridan, commander-in-chief of the Western troops, to arrange an Indian-style buffalo hunt for him: an extremely difficult and dangerous kind of hunt, with a high risk of being gored. So, on January 13 the train made a stop at North Platte, Nebraska, where the expedition landed and was joined by two heroes of the West: General Custer (on the left of the photograph) and Buffalo Bill Cody (on the right). Accompanied by Sheridan and with an escort of fifty cavalry, the party made camp on the bank of the Red Willow River. The hunt was led by Sioux Chief Striped Tail with one hundred of his warriors. The next day the hunters were up and off to the hunt. The Grand Duke was armed only with his Smith & Wesson. If we can believe Custer's account of the story, the Prince was a better horseman than marksman, and during their first chase he emptied his revolver wildly, missing his buffalo but shooting his horse through the head. Saddled up on a new mount, he exercised a bit more restraint and succeeded in bringing down a big bison, thus earning prestige for himself and for the Smith & Wesson revolver.

.44-caliber bullet mold.

.44-caliber Russian Smith & Wesson No. 3 Russian Third Model revolver, equipped with a short detachable walnut butt with a double metallic pin and a milled screw. This butt, first perfected for the Second Model, allows the revolver to change into a short rifle, giving greater stability while

shooting. This revolver was manufactured by Smith & Wesson in Springfield, Massachusetts, from 1874 to 1878. The Russian government bought 41,138. Turkey and Japan, in latent conflict with Russia, also made contracts with Smith & Wesson: Turkey, for

Original cleaning rod.

5,000 and Japan, 1,000. With 13,500 revolvers destined for the civilian market, there were, in all, 60,638 Smith & Wesson No. 3 Russian Third Models manufactured. The removable shoulder butts were designed for the civilian market.

Original box of 50 .44-caliber Smith & Wesson Russian cartridges.

50 .44 CAL. S&W. RUSSIAN,
CENTRAL-FIRE CARTRIDGES

TRADE
U.M.C.
MARK

.44 S&W
RUSSIAN
MODEL

23 GRS. POWDER
246 GRS BULLET

MANUFACTURED BY
THE UNION METALLIC CARTRIDGE Co.
BRIDGEPORT, CONN., U.S.A.

Smith & Wesson No. 3 New Model.
Manufactured from 1878 to 1912.
Quantity manufactured: 35,796.
Single action.
.38-44-caliber S&W.
Six-shot.
Downward-hinged frame.
Simultaneous break-open extractor.
6 ½-inch round ribbed barrel.
The Target model is shown here.

Smith & Wesson .38 Baby Russian First Model.
Manufactured from 1876 to 1877.
Quantity manufactured: 25,548.
Single action.
.38-caliber S&W.
Five-shot grooved cylinder.
Downward-hinged frame.
Simultaneous break-open extractor.
3 ¼- inch round ribbed barrel.

circumstance had placed him in the Confederate camp. Beaten black and blue by a band of Yankees who had tried to kill his adopted father and imprison his mother and sister, Jesse James could think of nothing but revenge. He joined Bill Anderson's Black Flag Brigade, a merciless Confederate guerilla outfit operating in Missouri and Kansas. When the South was defeated in 1865, Jesse James was eighteen years old. Though wanting to return to normal life, he was greeted by the authorities with gunshots. Seriously wounded, he barely managed to escape. The die was cast. Jesse James became the most vicious of the "lost soldiers" of the old South. The press in the North turned him into a monster. For Southerners, he was always the "Brigand with a golden heart." During his long rebellious career from 1865 to 1882, Jesse James used many different weapons. A photograph taken shortly after the war shows him carrying two cap-lock Colts, probably 1860 Army models. Later, he acquired a magnificent Smith & Wesson .45 Schofield, which he was wearing in his holster the day he was traitorously shot down by Bob Ford.

Smith & Wesson .38 Baby Russian Second Model.
Manufactured from 1877 to 1891.
Quantity manufactured: 108,255.
Single action.
.38-caliber S&W.
Five-shot, grooved cylinder.
Downward-hinged frame.
New Model simultaneous extractor.
4-inch round ribbed barrel.

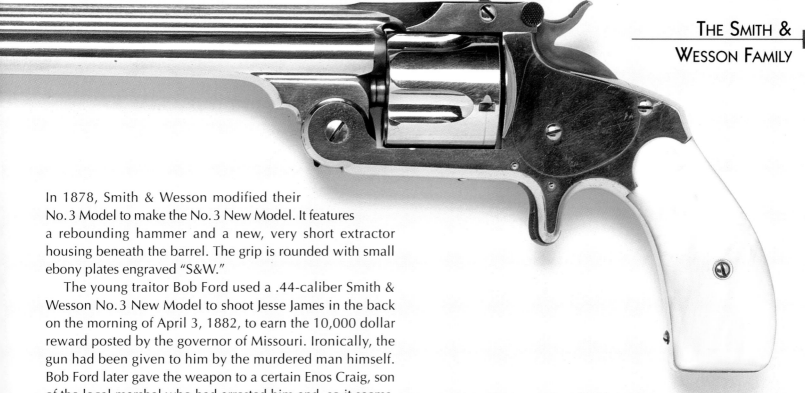

In 1878, Smith & Wesson modified their No. 3 Model to make the No. 3 New Model. It features a rebounding hammer and a new, very short extractor housing beneath the barrel. The grip is rounded with small ebony plates engraved "S&W."

The young traitor Bob Ford used a .44-caliber Smith & Wesson No. 3 New Model to shoot Jesse James in the back on the morning of April 3, 1882, to earn the 10,000 dollar reward posted by the governor of Missouri. Ironically, the gun had been given to him by the murdered man himself. Bob Ford later gave the weapon to a certain Enos Craig, son of the local marshal who had arrested him and, so it seems, treated him well. In 1900, Craig, out of money, sold the revolver to a citizen of Baltimore, who in turn sold it to somebody else. As for Bob Ford, he opened a saloon after being released from prison, where he was killed in 1892 by a fan of Jesse James.

Jesse James, one of the most notorious outlaws in the annals of Americana, was no ordinary criminal but an honorable bandit of sorts. At the beginning of the Civil War, he was but a teenager. The hazards of geography and

Smith & Wesson No. 3 Schofield
Second Model.
Manufactured from
1876 to1877.
Quantity manufactured: 5,934.
Single action.
.45-caliber Schofield center-fire.
Six-shot.
Downward-hinged frame.
Simultaneous break-open
extractor.
8-inch round ribbed barrel.

In early 1870, Colonel George Schofield, of the 10th Cavalry, made an improvement to the Smith & Wesson American No. 3 First Model revolver by reinforcing the barrel-latch. The cylinder-block was modified, as well as the extractor mechanism, which used a cam system instead of a racking one. The clip on the barrel latch was more solid than on the original

model. This revolver could also chamber a new cartridge. The .45 Schofield (future .45 Government) is not as powerful as the .45 Colt. It was designed to conquer the potential military market, but when the first perfected models were ready in 1873, the American army had already chosen the .45-caliber Colt 1873 Single-Action Army. Nonetheless, in September 1874, the army ordered 3,000 Schofields at $13.50 apiece, which were delivered the following year. The total number manufactured in 1875 did not exceed 3,035 (of which 3,000 were for the army). A second model featuring a new clip latch (recognizable by its checkered and hemispherical grip) was first manufactured in 1876. In all, 5,934 revolvers were manufactured from 1876 to 1877, of which 5,285 went to the army. The military models carry the army inspector's brand on the left-plate of the grip.

The cartridge-belt next to the original military holster and saddle-bag is designed for rifle cartridges.

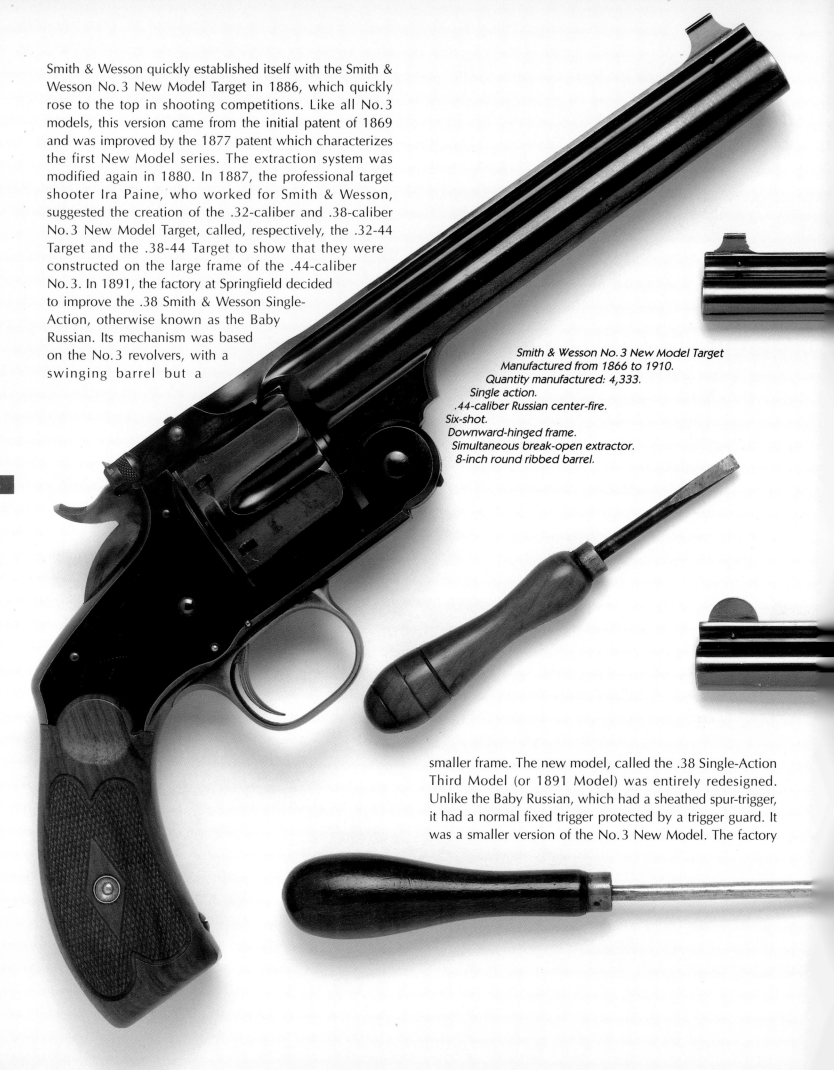

Smith & Wesson quickly established itself with the Smith & Wesson No. 3 New Model Target in 1886, which quickly rose to the top in shooting competitions. Like all No. 3 models, this version came from the initial patent of 1869 and was improved by the 1877 patent which characterizes the first New Model series. The extraction system was modified again in 1880. In 1887, the professional target shooter Ira Paine, who worked for Smith & Wesson, suggested the creation of the .32-caliber and .38-caliber No. 3 New Model Target, called, respectively, the .32-44 Target and the .38-44 Target to show that they were constructed on the large frame of the .44-caliber No. 3. In 1891, the factory at Springfield decided to improve the .38 Smith & Wesson Single-Action, otherwise known as the Baby Russian. Its mechanism was based on the No. 3 revolvers, with a swinging barrel but a

Smith & Wesson No. 3 New Model Target
Manufactured from 1866 to 1910.
Quantity manufactured: 4,333.
Single action.
.44-caliber Russian center-fire.
Six-shot.
Downward-hinged frame.
Simultaneous break-open extractor.
8-inch round ribbed barrel.

smaller frame. The new model, called the .38 Single-Action Third Model (or 1891 Model) was entirely redesigned. Unlike the Baby Russian, which had a sheathed spur-trigger, it had a normal fixed trigger protected by a trigger guard. It was a smaller version of the No. 3 New Model. The factory

attributed a serial number to it, starting with 1 in 1891 and finishing at 28,107 at the end of manufacturing in 1911. In 1893, the factory produced a conversion model of this revolver for target shooting competitions – it was a one-barrel, single-shot, revolver with no cylinder. The supplementary barrel carried the same number as the revolver. The set was available in .22, .32 S&W, and .38 S&W calibers, with single-shot barrels of 6, 8, or 10 inches. A special grip for target shooting was also added.

Smith & Wesson .38 Single-Action Third Model.
Manufactured from 1891 to 1911.
Quantity manufactured: 28,107.
Single action.
.44-caliber S&W (also exists in .32- and .22-caliber).
Five-shot.
Downward-hinged frame.
Simultaneous break-open extractor.
6-inch round ribbed barrel.

THE COLT PEACEMAKER AND ITS COMPETITORS

There is no more illustrious revolver than the Colt Peacemaker. There is also no example of such an old weapon in production for such a long time in the original factory. The factory archives have kept records of all private sales of Colt Peacemakers. There we find the names of Theodore Roosevelt, Buffalo Bill, Billy the Kid, Wyatt Earp, Pat Garrett, Allan Pinkerton, Jesse James, John Wesley Hardin, Heck Thomas, Calamity Jane, and Bat Masterson. General Patton remained faithful all his life to his first Peacemaker, which had a beautiful ivory-plated grip. Even when he had become a specialist in armored combat at the end of the Second World War, his Peacemaker never left his side. He bought it in Texas, where, in 1916, he served as a lieutenant in the U.S. army, just after the raid on Pancho Villa—himself a Peacemaker fan. Thanks to westerns, this beautiful and powerful revolver has become an archetype. The filmmakers who have put this revolver in the holsters and the hands of generations of cowboys, sheriffs, outlaws, and soldiers of the American cavalry, without paying too much attention to plausibility or chronology, had all the excuses. The Colt Peacemaker is incredibly photogenic and no other revolver lends itself so well to the Hollywood ritual of the quick draw and fanning: thumb-slapping the hammer to achieve machine-gun speed. The Colt Peacemaker appeals to people's imagination everywhere because it has transcended its purely American origins and become a symbol of adventure in the vast realms of fiction.

A Colt Civilian Model with a relatively short barrel (5 ½- inch) and an antler-bone grip. It is resting on a genuine embroidered suede cowboy shirt from the 1880s.

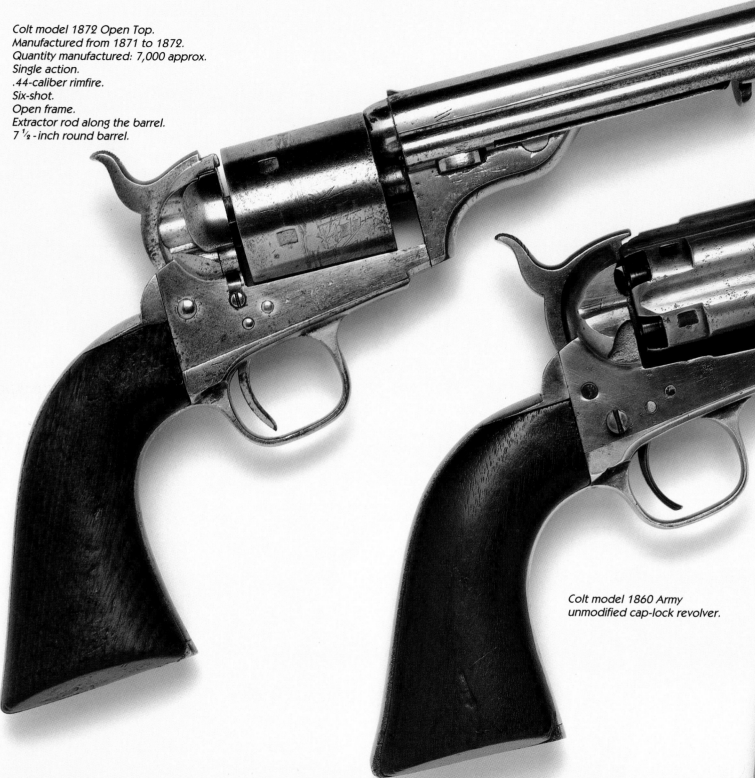

Colt model 1872 Open Top.
Manufactured from 1871 to 1872.
Quantity manufactured: 7,000 approx.
Single action.
.44-caliber rimfire.
Six-shot.
Open frame.
Extractor rod along the barrel.
7 ½ - inch round barrel.

Colt model 1860 Army
unmodified cap-lock revolver.

Shortly before his death in 1862, Samuel Colt asked his closest collaborator, Elisha Root, to take over control of the company. Root died three years later. Having inherited almost all of her husband's property, Mrs. Elisabeth Colt made her brother Richard Javis president of the company, a position he held successfully until 1901. His principal partner was General William B. Franklin, who had won his stars in the Union army during the Civil War and maintained useful relations with the War Department.

Three engineers completed the team: C.B. Richards, F.A. Thuer, and William Mason. All three worked on developing firearms for the new, revolutionary metal-case cartridge. They focused first on adapting the old Colt cap-lock revolvers to the new cartridges.

The Thuer conversion, whose patent was granted on September 15, 1868, was based on the Rollin White patent that had previously given Smith & Wesson its monopoly on bored-through cylinder revolver

Thuer conversion, Colt 1860 Army.
Manufactured from 1869 to 1872.
Quantity manufactured: 5,000 approx.
Single action.
.44-caliber Thuer.
Six-shot.
Open frame.
Round shortened barrel.

production. It used a special cartridge loaded at the front of the cylinder, behind a conversion ring. The modified cylinder and the original percussion cylinder were interchangeable so that the weapon could be used with caps or the new metal-case cartridges. The Colt factory continued with these modifications for clients who owned percussion revolvers long after the commercialization of the Colt 1873 Army Peacemaker. In all, 46,000 Colt revolvers were modified at the Hartford factory to

accommodate different types of metal-case cartridges. In 1871, the Colt factory began manufacturing the 1872 Open Top—a transition model. The Colt 1860 Army's mechanism and open top frame were kept, but a new bored-through cylinder made for metal-case rimfire cartridges was added. The rammer lever was dropped. The cylinder console and hammer were modified. It also had an ejector rod on the barrel side. This 1872 model was the bridge between the old cap-lock models and the future solid-frame center-fire Colt 1873 Army Peacemaker.

At the end of 1872, William Mason, one of the chief engineers at the Colt factory, conceived and manufactured the prototype of a new revolver for the .45 Colt (also called the ".45 Long Colt") center-fire percussion cartridge that had been created that same year.

Essentially, the new revolver conserved the solid single-action mechanism that had made Colt's revolvers famous since the 1849 Dragoon No. 2. It also kept the form and construction of the Colt Walker model 1847 Army grip, but its solid frame made it much sturdier than the old open-frame patterns. The large non-rebounding hammer has a fixed pin and a half-cock notch safety feature. Spent cases are ejected sequentially by a spring-loaded rod in a case on the lower right side of the barrel. The ejector's finger-piece projects under the barrel to the left, allowing

the firer to eject spent cases while rotating the cylinder with the firing hand. The base pin is fastened with a screw on the first 150,000 manufactured and then, after 1893, by a latch patented by Mason. This magnificent revolver was bought by the U.S. army in 1873 and is officially called the Colt model 1873

Colt model 1873 Single-Action Army (Artillery Model).
Same characteristics as the Cavalry Model, except a 5 ½-inch barrel.

Colt model 1873 Single-Action Army (Cavalry Model).
Manufactured since 1873.
Quantity manufactured from 1873 to 1940: 310,386.
Single action.
.44-caliber Colt center-fire.
Six-shot.
Solid frame.
Extractor rod along the barrel.
7 ½-inch round barrel.

Single-Action Army. It was equally well known as the Peacemaker, Six-Shooter, or Frontier, the latter referring to those models manufactured in .44-40 caliber Winchester. In time, this revolver was produced in a wide range of calibers and finishes. There were five lengths of barrel: 7½ inches for the

Cavalry Model, 5 ½ inches for the Artillery Model, 4 ¾ inches for the Civilian Model, 2 ½ inches for the Sheriff Model, and 16 inches for the Buntline. For use in the military and on the frontier, it had the advantage of being both extremely simple and extremely robust. In its most usual caliber (.45 Colt), it was to be the most powerful revolver on the market for a long time.

Colt model 1873 Single-Action Army (Civilian Model). Same characteristics as the Cavalry Model, except a 4 ¾-inch barrel.

The great cowboy adventure began at the end of the Civil War in 1865 and lasted for twenty glorious years. During the war, wild Texan longhorns had multiplied freely. The re-establishment of communications and the demand for beef in the North, South, and West suddenly offered enormous market potential. Texan ranchers were quick to seize the opportunity, aided by ranch workers selected from the ranks of Confederate army riders. Excellent horsemen, hardened by war and deprivation, they became cowboys. Riding herd for several months of the year, they drove cattle from watering hole to watering hole until they reached their destination, the great railway yards from where cattle were shipped off to slaughterhouses across the country. The hardships of the long drive, with the dangers

posed by rustlers who stole their cattle and farmers who blocked their way with barbed wire, gave birth to the great and sometimes bloody cowboy epic. On a long drive the herd forms a sort of elongated, waving tactical unit. Leaving Texas in early spring, when the grass was sure to be long, the herd would snake along at about fifteen miles a day, with cowboys riding ahead and behind. Old-timers' tales, both comic and tragic, abound. Among all the dangers of the trail, the worst, after the cattle being driven mad by the heat, thirst, or a storm, was the Indian. The temptation to steal food or to settle scores with these evil white men was too great for the Sioux, Comanches, or the Cheyennes. When forces were unequal, the cowboys' only salvation was in their revolvers and in flight.

The revolution brought about by the development of the metal-case cartridge took much longer than one would imagine. First it was necessary to manufacture new guns in sufficient quantities and then to make gun users, most of whom were often far from urban centers, aware of them. In the West, old habits die hard, and the new arms were often looked upon with mistrust. They were expensive, and men who were comfortable with their "old" cap-lock revolvers saw no reason why they should give them up for some newfangled contraption. The first rimfire metal-case cartridges were much weaker than the powerful charges used in the cap-lock revolvers. People were also afraid that they would find themselves short of ammunition; one

could always find gunpowder, lead, and caps in the little general store, but the guns using metal-case cartridges could chamber only their exact caliber. It is easy to understand, therefore, why the "old" revolvers continued to be used long after the appearance of the new metal-case cartridges. The cowboys appreciated the fact that they could save money on a new purchase by converting their "old" revolvers rather than buying new ones, particularly because some conversions—the new cylinder and the original percussion cylinder—were interchangeable. The Remington Company, which, since 1858, made its most robust percussion revolver using a closed frame, created many conversion systems in different calibers.

Remington conversion model 1863 Army.
Single action.
.44-caliber center-fire.
Six-shot.
Solid frame.
Octagonal barrel.

Remington conversion model 1863 Army.
Single action.
.44-caliber rimfire.
Six-shot.
Solid frame.
Octagonal barrel.

In the open competition to create metal-case cartridges, the Remington Company found itself outgunned by Colt, who in 1873 launched the Single-Action Army (the Peacemaker) in both the military and civilian markets to immediate success. After offering several conversions of its "old" cap-lock models, the Remington factory in Ilion, New York, released an original metal-case cartridge revolver, the Single-Action Army, in 1875. About 25,000 were manufactured between 1875 and 1889 in three center-fire calibers: .44 Remington, .44-40 Winchester, and .45 Schofield, otherwise known as the .45 Government. This revolver could not compete with the Peacemaker, of which 130,000 had already been sold by 1889. It does not seem to have been bought by the American army, but 1,300 nickel-plated 1875 model revolvers were bought by the Interior Department to arm Indian police officers on the reservations. The Remington Company also obtained an order from the Mexican government, and 10,000 more were purchased by the Egyptian government. One of the most notorious bearers of the 1875 model was the outlaw Frank James. He was carrying serial number 5116 when he surrendered, and his brother, Jesse James, also used a Remington 1875—serial number 559.

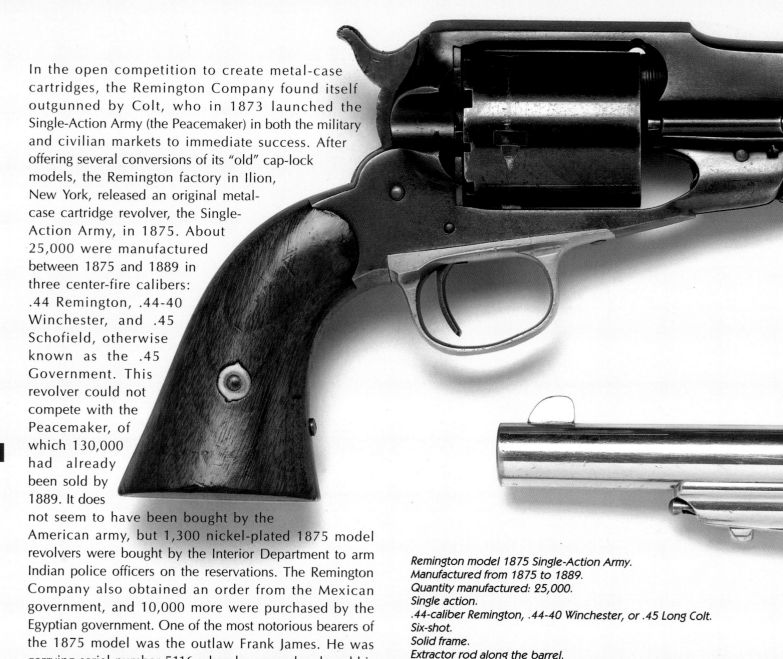

Remington model 1875 Single-Action Army.
Manufactured from 1875 to 1889.
Quantity manufactured: 25,000.
Single action.
.44-caliber Remington, .44-40 Winchester, or .45 Long Colt.
Six-shot.
Solid frame.
Extractor rod along the barrel.
7 ½ - inch round barrel.

Remington conversion New Model 1863.
Manufactured since 1870.
Single action.
.46-caliber rimfire.
Six-shot.
Solid frame.
No extractor rod; the rammer has been conserved.
8-inch octagonal barrel.

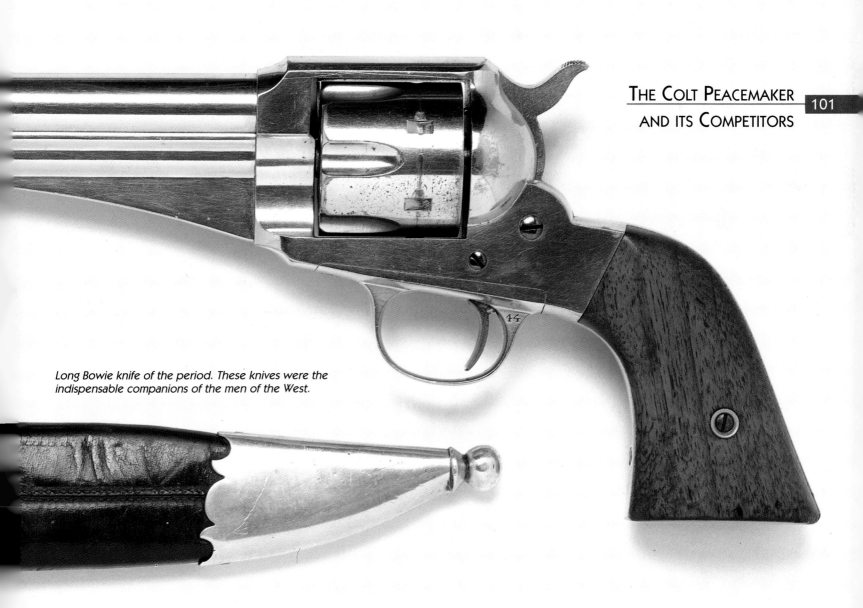

Long Bowie knife of the period. These knives were the
indispensable companions of the men of the West.

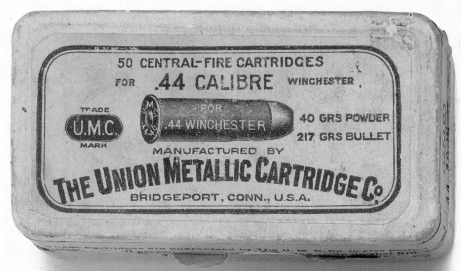

Original .44-40-caliber Winchester cartridge box.

Merwin Hulbert model 1876 Army No. 1.
Manufactured from 1876 to 1880.
Quantity manufactured: 15,000 approx.
Single action.
.44-40-caliber WCF.
Six-shot.
Open frame.
Simultaneous extractor.
7 ½ - inch round barrel.

Merwin Hulbert and Company, whose head office was in New York, was not an arms manufacturer. The company had guns made for it, under the name of Merwin Hulbert, in order to have exclusive rights. Several of its firearms were manufactured by Hopkins & Allen in Norwich, Connecticut. The 1876 Army No. 1 was a single-action open-frame revolver with a unique auto-ejector mechanism. Once unlocked, the barrel as well as its console rotated a quarter turn, escaping the dovetailing mechanism that fastened them to the frame. Pushed through the spiral groove on the cylinder-pin, they are kept from advancing while the spent cases, held in by a flange, are ejected. While this system is at once

Forehand & Wadsworth Old Model Army.
Manufactured around 1875.
Quantity manufactured: several thousand.
Single action.
.44-caliber Russian.
Six-shot.
Solid frame.
7 ½-inch round barrel.

more complicated and less effective than the S&W No. 3, the revolvers are very well constructed. Another competitor of the Peacemaker was the Forehand & Wadsworth revolver. Sullivan Forehand was manager of Allan & Wheelock, a well-known manufacturer of pepperboxes and pocket revolvers. He married the daughter of Ethan Allen and had two sons who both became gun-makers. His brother-in-law, Henry C. Wadsworth, a former officer, married another of Ethan Allen's daughters. When Allen died in 1871, the company he had founded became Forehand & Wadsworth. Much later, in 1902, after the death of the two associates, the company was absorbed by Hopkins & Allen, who, as we have just seen, was the manufacturer of Merwin Hulbert's revolvers. Everything comes around full circle.

103

Winchester tools for reloading cartridges.

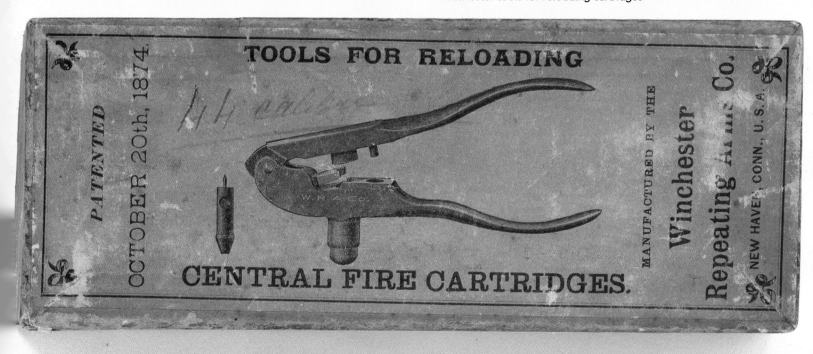

SKINNER & DUNN.

The saloon was the mythical center of small towns in the West during the cattle empire epoch. One of the most famous towns was Dodge City, the "Queen of the Cow-Towns," the "Babylon of the Frontier," associated with legendary sheriffs and outlaws like Bat Masterson, Bill Tilgham, Clay Allison, and Wyatt Earp. Every winter the towns prepared for the arrival of the cattle herds, cowboys, and people hoping to get hold of some of the money here. For several months, from spring to summer, the cattle drives emptied into the towns. Cowboys ruled here and often numbered up to a thousand. As soon as the cattle were sold, they would be paid for the year. After a visit to the barber and the public bath-house, buying some clothes to replace their old worn-out ones, they would spend what remained on whiskey, women, and gambling. Hoodlums, peddlars, prostitutes, and snake-oil salesmen, attracted by their money, would come into town in droves. From time to time, gunfire would ring out, revolvers used to settle a score, usually making more noise than shedding blood. Sometimes, someone would have to lay low for a while to heal from wounds and every once in a while some unfortunate would be killed. According to the custom, he would be buried with his boots and sometimes even his six-shooter.

In 1888, financial difficulties forced the Remington family to come to an agreement with its creditors and cede direction of the company to Marcellus Hartley. The company changed its name to Remington Arms Company. The new boss concentrated on, among other projects, the development of handguns. To compete effectively with Colt, he decided he would have to do better, and so he came out with the 1890 Single-Action Army, whose appearance, not to mention its name, was very much like that of the Peacemaker. In spite of the gun's qualities, it proved a complete failure commercially. Between 1891 and 1894, production hardly surpassed 2,000; consequently, finding one today is very rare. Meanwhile, Merwin Hulbert put into production a revolver that was along

the same lines as his 1876 model, but with a solid-frame design which gave it

Remington model 1890 Single-Action Army.
Manufactured from 1891 to 1894.
Quantity manufactured: 2,000.
Single action.
.45-caliber WCF.
Six-shot.
Solid frame.

Extractor rod along the barrel.
5 ½-inch round barrel.

extra sturdiness. Moderately successful on the market, it was the gun of preference of Bud Ledbetter, the Federal Marshal who scoured Oklahoma for the infamous Judge Parker. In 1880, Ledbetter was intrigued by this revolver, which he discovered at a local gunsmith's.

"I chose my gun from twenty-three others," he wrote in his memoirs. "I tested them for four days. Then I decided on the Merwin Hulbert Army, .44-40 caliber, number 6411/971 because it performed the best. Today, twenty years later, I've shot

Merwin Hulbert model 1876 Army No. 2.
Manufactured about 1880.
Quantity manufactured: several thousand.
Single action.
.44-40-caliber WCF.
Six-shot.
Solid frame.
Simultaneous extractor.
7 ½-inch round
barrel.

thousands of shells, I've had it re-plated with nickel and I carry it everywhere I go."

A third competitor for the Colt Peacemaker was the short-barreled Schofield Model which, like the two others presented here, has a special nickel finish.

Smith & Wesson No. 3 Schofield First Model.
Manufactured from 1876 to 1877.
Quantity manufactured: 3,035.
Single action.
.45-caliber Schofield center-fire.
Six-shot.
Downward-hinged frame.
Simultaneous break-open extractor.
4 ¾-inch barrel.

The development of target shooting led the directors of the Colt Company to offer a special version of the 1873 Single-Action Army, the Flat-top Target Model, which featured a bead and an adjustable fore sight. In all, 925 were manufactured between 1888 and 1896, in many different calibers. As demand grew, Colt decided to create a special model for target shooting; this was the Bisley Model, manufactured from 1894 to 1915 in eighteen different calibers. It was named after the famous British firing range. The Bisley was easily recognizable by the pronounced angle of the well-shaped handle. It differed from the Peacemaker in its hammer spur and large trigger, more open trigger guard,

and the hammer stirrup that replaced the roller between the main spring and the hammer. The barrel was manufactured in many lengths from 4¾ to 7½ inches. The Bisley's users were not exclusively confined to target shooters: John Thompson, a well-known Arizona sheriff, carried a .32-20-caliber Bisley.

Embossed leather gauntlet used by cowboys to protect their wrists when working with cattle.

Colt Bisley Model Single-Action Army.
Manufactured from 1894 to 1915.
Quantity manufactured: 44,350.
Single action.
.44-40-caliber WCF (also exists in other calibers).
Six-shot.
Solid frame.
Extractor rod along the barrel.
7 ½-inch barrel (also offered with barrel lengths from
4 ¾-inch to 7 ½-inch).

AT THE CARD TABLE

In the West, the professional gambler—sometimes a woman—is a character almost as indispensable as the cowboy, Indian, sheriff, and outlaw. Poker games would often end in a cloud of gunpowder and nobody would come to the table without a small gun hidden in their pouch, belt, or purse. Compact pistols remained popular even after small inexpensive revolvers became available, as these were more difficult to hide. Named after their designer, Philadelphian gunsmith Henry Deringer (1786-1868), the word deringer entered the language and came to describe any and all pocket pistols. Deringer became famous for his superb single-shot, muzzle-loaded .41- and .44-caliber cap-lock pocket pistols. These guns were remarkably well made, perfectly balanced, and elegant. It was with a genuine Deringer that the actor John Wilkes Booth assassinated President Lincoln on April 14, 1865, in the Ford Theatre in Washington, to avenge the defeat of the Confederate South. For professional gamblers and ladies of ill repute, the Deringer was challenged only by small-caliber pocket revolvers, such as the Colt New Line models, which had the advantage of being able to fire several shots consecutively.

Card table of the period. Next to the cards, dice, and a whiskey flask, at the top, sits a small Smith & Wesson .22 First Model (third type), nickel plated, engraved, and with mother-of-pearl plates: a classic of card players. In the middle is a rare Smith & Wesson .32 R.F. New Model, nickel and gold plated, engraved, and with mother-of-pearl plates; this gun was often sold openly in saloons. At the bottom is a Remington Smoot .41 R.F. New Model, nickel plated and engraved. Approximately 10,000 of these guns were manufactured.

At the end of the 1860s, the period that saw the emergence of metal-case cartridges, many manufacturers started making pocket pistols with interesting and often perplexing shapes and mechanisms.

Chuchu Pistol.
Manufactured around 1870.
Double action.
.22-caliber rimfire.
Four-shot.
Break-open barrels.
Rotating firing pin.
1 ³⁄₄-inch barrels.

Remington Rider.
Manufactured from 1871 to 1888.
Quantity manufactured: 10,000 approx.
Single-action repeating mechanism.
.32-caliber rimfire.
Five-shot.
Tubular cartridge underneath the barrel and a loader next to the hammer.
3-inch octagonal barrel.

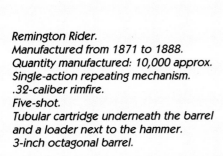

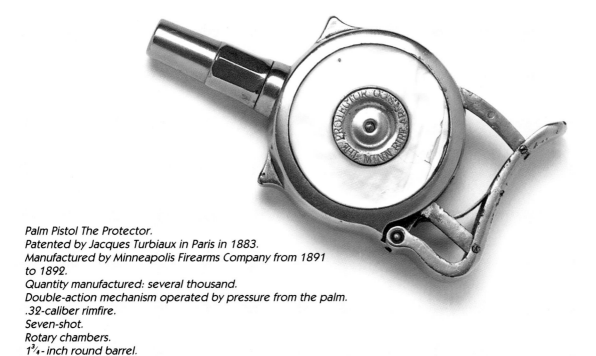

Palm Pistol The Protector.
Patented by Jacques Turbiaux in Paris in 1883.
Manufactured by Minneapolis Firearms Company from 1891
to 1892.
Quantity manufactured: several thousand.
Double-action mechanism operated by pressure from the palm.
.32-caliber rimfire.
Seven-shot.
Rotary chambers.
1³/₄-inch round barrel.

Unique Palm Pistol.
Manufactured by Shattuck Arms Company, Hatfield, Massachusetts,
from 1907 to 1915.
Quantity manufactured: several thousand.
Double-action mechanism operated by pressure from the palm.
.32-caliber rimfire.
Four-shot.
Ascending chambers.
1¹/₂-inch barrel.

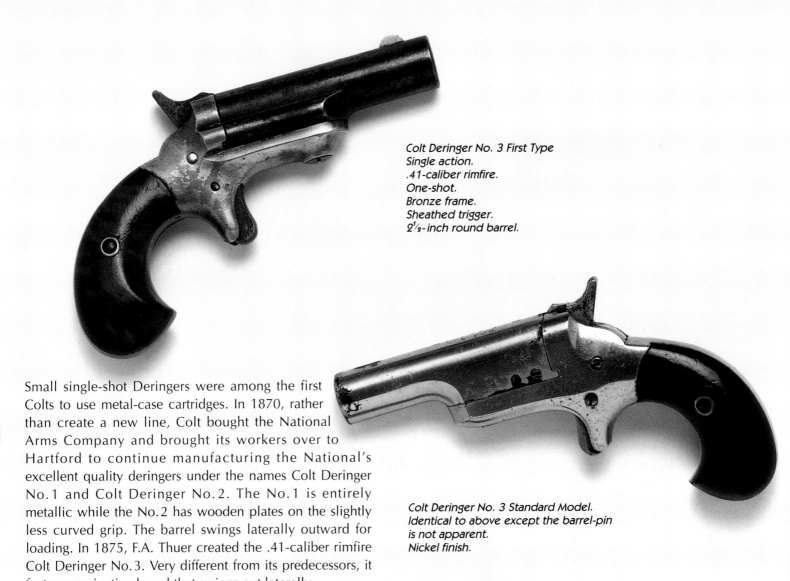

Colt Deringer No. 3 First Type
Single action.
.41-caliber rimfire.
One-shot.
Bronze frame.
Sheathed trigger.
2½-inch round barrel.

Colt Deringer No. 3 Standard Model.
Identical to above except the barrel-pin
is not apparent.
Nickel finish.

Small single-shot Deringers were among the first Colts to use metal-case cartridges. In 1870, rather than create a new line, Colt bought the National Arms Company and brought its workers over to Hartford to continue manufacturing the National's excellent quality deringers under the names Colt Deringer No. 1 and Colt Deringer No. 2. The No. 1 is entirely metallic while the No. 2 has wooden plates on the slightly less curved grip. The barrel swings laterally outward for loading. In 1875, F.A. Thuer created the .41-caliber rimfire Colt Deringer No. 3. Very different from its predecessors, it features a pivoting barrel that swings out laterally.

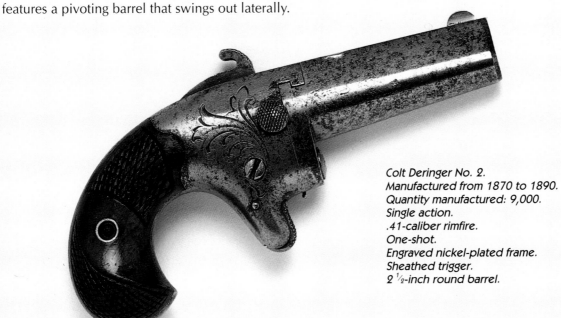

Colt Deringer No. 2.
Manufactured from 1870 to 1890.
Quantity manufactured: 9,000.
Single action.
.41-caliber rimfire.
One-shot.
Engraved nickel-plated frame.
Sheathed trigger.
2 ½-inch round barrel.

Remington-Beals 1857 Pocket First Type.
Manufactured from 1857 to 1859.
Quantity manufactured: 4,500.
Single action.
.31-caliber percussion.
Five-shot.
Solid frame.
Sheathed trigger.
3-inch octagonal barrel.

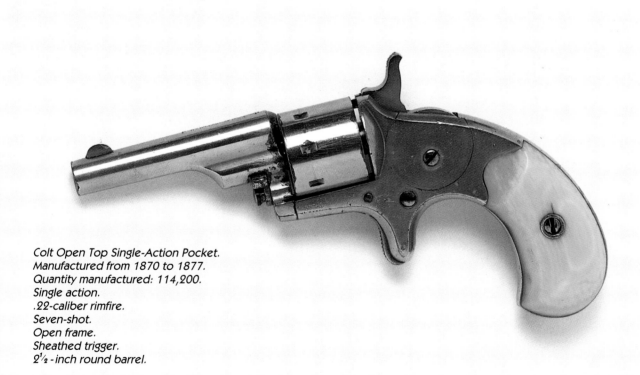

Colt Open Top Single-Action Pocket.
Manufactured from 1870 to 1877.
Quantity manufactured: 114,200.
Single action.
.22-caliber rimfire.
Seven-shot.
Open frame.
Sheathed trigger.
2$\frac{1}{2}$-inch round barrel.

In the new gold rush towns and cattle-trading centers that sprang up in a few days, saloons and gambling dens were the first businesses to open their doors. After weeks in the mountains mining for gold, or after months on the trail, driving enormous herds of longhorn, gold miners and cowboys hungered for pleasure, women, whiskey, and gambling. Croupiers, poker players, and easy women, attracted by the cowboys' money, arrived from Kansas City or New Orleans, and happiness prevailed every evening in the saloons. After visiting the barber, the public baths, and the iron-monger-outfitters to buy new clothes, the young riders, their Colts by their side, entered the bar and sat down at the gaming tables. The poker games, often led by professionals, frequently ended with shots from a revolver or deringer—the girls' and pro-fessional players' favorite weapon. Sometimes the sheriffs were also professional players, like Bat Masterson or Wyatt Earp, and it was difficult to tell, when meeting them in a saloon, whether they were there as bandits or lawmen.

*Williamson Single-Shot Deringer.
Manufactured from 1866 to 1870.
Quantity manufactured: 3,000.
Single action.
.41-caliber rimfire and
percussion cap lock.
The barrel slides
forward for loading.
2 ½ -inch round
barrel.*

1888 in two calibers (.22 and .32) with different characteristics (five .22-caliber barrel lengths and four .32-caliber barrel lengths), it was moderately. successful with a total production of about 25,000. Not a pepperbox, as its barrels were fixed, its double-action ring trigger rotated the barrel block. In the same period, other manufacturers continued to make single-shot deringers, such as the one by Williamson, which featured an adaptor that allowed it to be used like an "old" muzzle-loaded cap-lock pistol but was ultimately designed to hold a cartridge of .41 rimfire.

Like many other large firearm manufacturers, Remington produced many pocket pistols in response to the growing demand for little handguns that could be easily placed in a pocket or hidden under clothes. After suffering a disappointment with its Zig-Zag pepperbox created in 1861, Remington looked with interest at the small multiple-barrelled pistols patented by William Elliot on May 29, 1860, and October 1, 1861. Manufactured from 1863 to

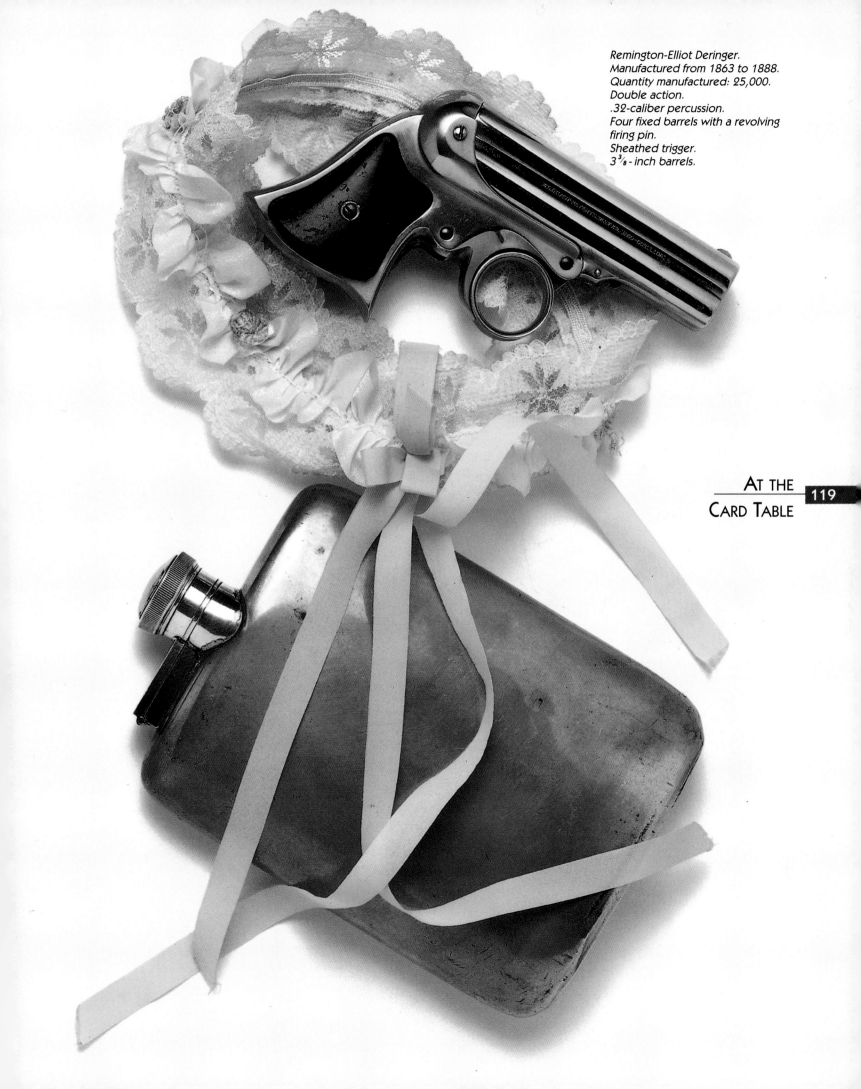

Remington-Elliot Deringer.
Manufactured from 1863 to 1888.
Quantity manufactured: 25,000.
Double action.
.32-caliber percussion.
Four fixed barrels with a revolving
firing pin.
Sheathed trigger.
$3\frac{3}{8}$ - inch barrels.

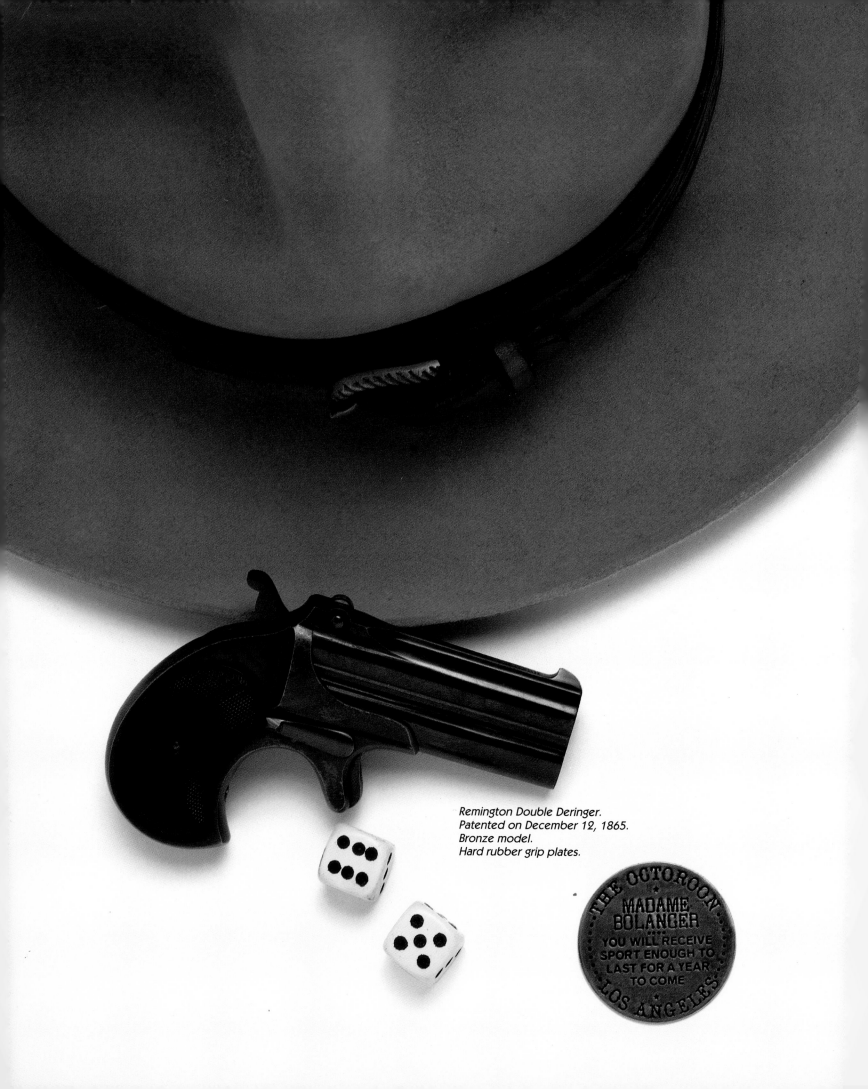

Remington Double Deringer.
Patented on December 12, 1865.
Bronze model.
Hard rubber grip plates.

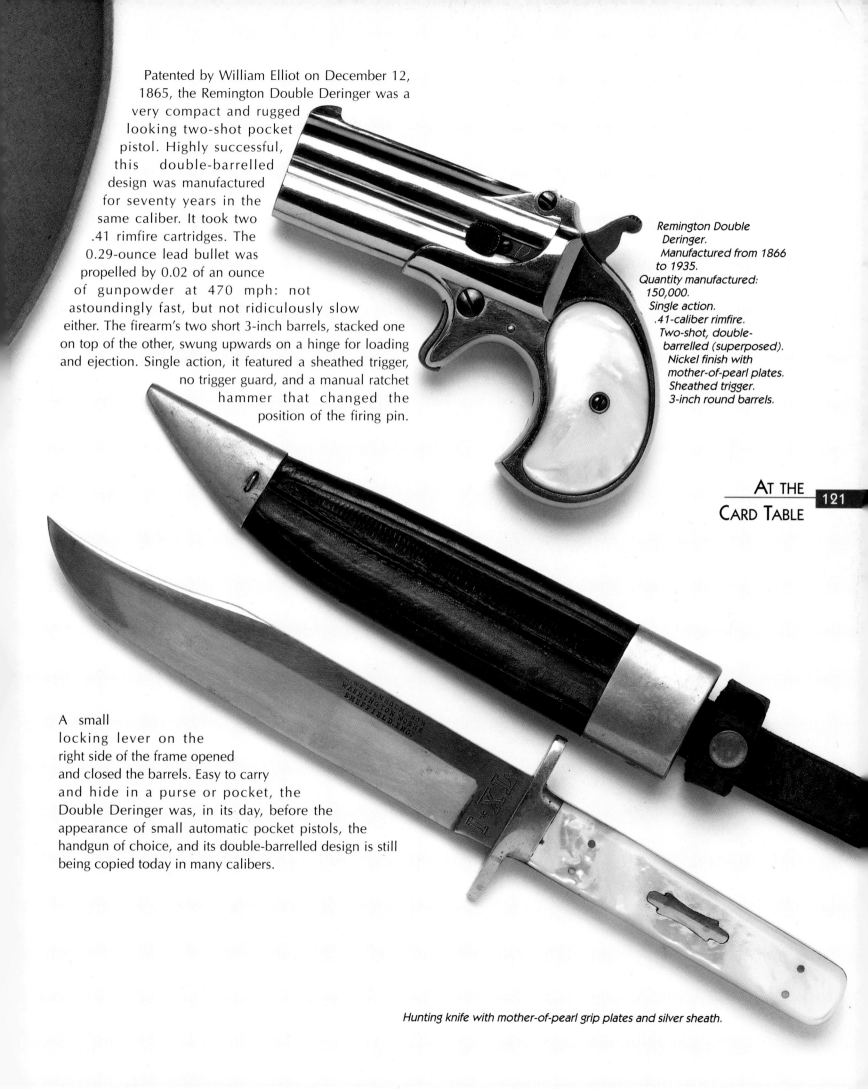

Patented by William Elliot on December 12, 1865, the Remington Double Deringer was a very compact and rugged looking two-shot pocket pistol. Highly successful, this double-barrelled design was manufactured for seventy years in the same caliber. It took two .41 rimfire cartridges. The 0.29-ounce lead bullet was propelled by 0.02 of an ounce of gunpowder at 470 mph: not astoundingly fast, but not ridiculously slow either. The firearm's two short 3-inch barrels, stacked one on top of the other, swung upwards on a hinge for loading and ejection. Single action, it featured a sheathed trigger, no trigger guard, and a manual ratchet hammer that changed the position of the firing pin.

Remington Double Deringer. Manufactured from 1866 to 1935. Quantity manufactured: 150,000. Single action. .41-caliber rimfire. Two-shot, double-barrelled (superposed). Nickel finish with mother-of-pearl plates. Sheathed trigger. 3-inch round barrels.

A small locking lever on the right side of the frame opened and closed the barrels. Easy to carry and hide in a purse or pocket, the Double Deringer was, in its day, before the appearance of small automatic pocket pistols, the handgun of choice, and its double-barrelled design is still being copied today in many calibers.

Hunting knife with mother-of-pearl grip plates and silver sheath.

Colt New Line
Single-Action Pocket Cal. .30.
Manufactured from
1874 to 1880.
Quantity manufactured:
11,000.
.30-caliber rimfire.
Five-shot.
Solid frame.
Sheathed trigger.
2 ¼-inch round barrel.

Colt New Line Single-Action Pocket Cal. .38.
Manufactured from 1874 to 1880.
Quantity manufactured: 5,500.
.38-caliber rimfire.
Five-shot.
Solid-frame.
Sheathed trigger.
3-inch round barrel.

Along with their metal-case Deringers, Colt soon manufactured pocket revolvers like the .41-caliber rimfire four-shot House Model Cloverleaf and the highly successful .22-caliber rimfire seven-shot Colt Open Top Single-Action Pocket, which weighed a mere 8 ounces. The latter was a great success, and 114,200 revolvers were produced in seven years. Soon after this revolver came out, William Mason, who had begun by working for

Remington, set up a series of New Line Single-Action Pocket revolvers in 1873 whose size varied according to the different calibers. Four frame sizes and five calibers were manufactured: the .22 rimfire (55,343 manufactured), the .30 rimfire (11,000), the .32 rimfire (22,000), the .38 rimfire (5,500), and the .41 rimfire (7,000).

Colt Open Top Single-Action Pocket.
Manufactured from 1870 to 1877.
Quantity manufactured: 114,200.
.22-caliber rimfire.
Seven-shot.
Open frame.
Sheathed trigger.
2 ½-inch round barrel.

Indian bead-bag from the nineteenth century.
Polychrome pearl design.

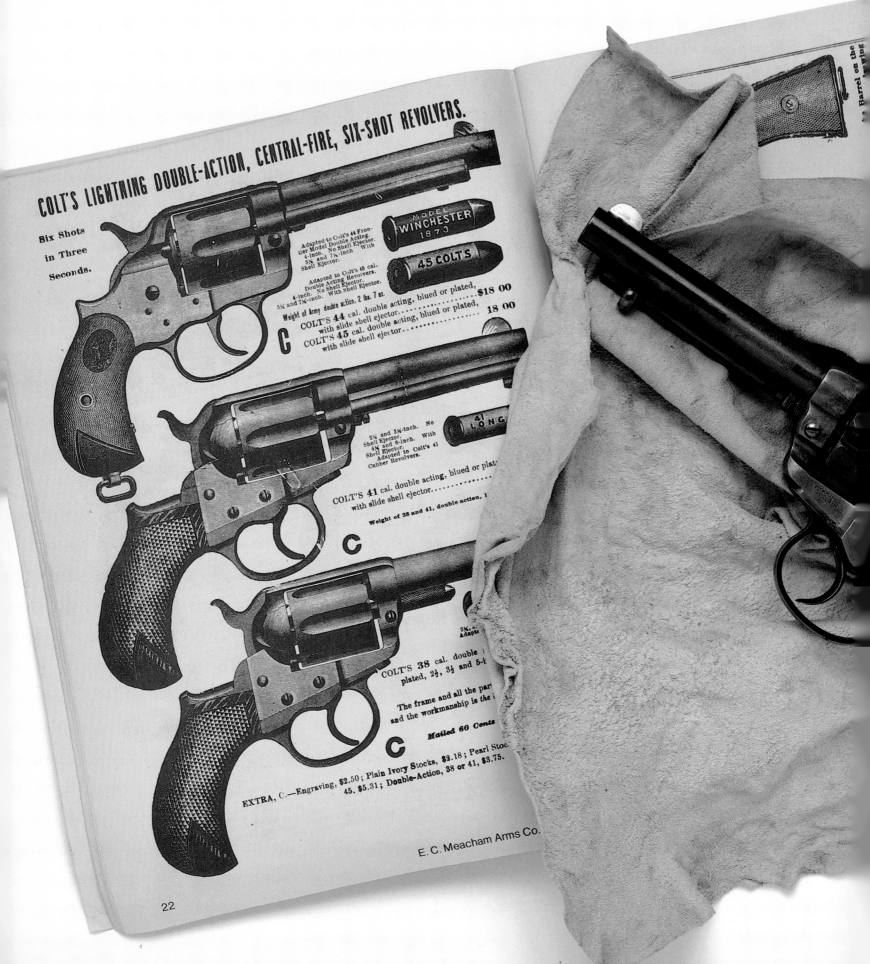

COLT'S LIGHTNING DOUBLE-ACTION, CENTRAL-FIRE, SIX-SHOT REVOLVERS.

Six Shots
in Three
Seconds.

Adapted to Colt's 44 Frontier Model Double Acting.
4-inch. No Shell Ejector.
5½ and 7½-inch. With Shell Ejector.

Adapted to Colt's 45 cal.
Double Acting Revolvers.
4-inch. No Shell Ejector.
5½ and 7½-inch. With Shell Ejector.

MODEL WINCHESTER 1873

45 COLT'S

Weight of Army double action, 2 lbs. 7 oz.

COLT'S **44** cal. double acting, blued or plated, ... $18 00
with slide shell ejector..........................
COLT'S **45** cal. double acting, blued or plated, ... 18 00
with slide shell ejector....................

C

2½ and 3½-inch. No
Shell Ejector.
4½ and 6-inch. With
Shell Ejector.
Adapted to Colt's 41
Caliber Revolvers.

41 LONG

COLT'S **41** cal. double acting, blued or plated,
with slide shell ejector....................

Weight of 38 and 41, double action,

C

2½,
Adapte

COLT'S **38** cal. double
plated, 2½, 3½ and 5-i

The frame and all the part
and the workmanship is the

Mailed 60 Cents

C

EXTRA, C.—Engraving, $2.50 ; Plain Ivory Stocks, $2.18 ; Pearl Stoc
45, $5.31 ; Double-Action, 38 or 41, $3.75.

E. C. Meacham Arms Co.

22

THE DAWN OF THE MODERN FIREARM

Despite his inventive flair, Samuel Colt did not live to see the advent of the metal-case cartridge, nor could he have predicted the great potential of double-action mechanisms. How could he have guessed, at his death in 1862, that his name would be later given to the famous automatic pistol? The father of the most celebrated Colt automatic pistol—the Colt .45—was a young genius named John M. Browning. His pistol, officially called the Colt .45 Model 1911 Automatic Pistol, was adopted by the American army in 1911. Close to a century later, it is still manufactured with different variations, though it is no longer used by the army.

Several other models, notably the first perfected American double-action revolver, the 1877 Lightning Model, paved the way for the Colt .45. Samuel Colt had always scorned double-action mechanisms, whose trigger resistance reduced shooting precision. He also believed that these revolvers were not as safe as the good, old-fashioned single actions. Even the great Sam Colt could not foresee that in the following decades, competitors and successors would invent a series of double-action mechanisms with greater shooting flexibility and reliable safety features. The Colt Lightning was very different from its predecessors.

Colt model 1877 Lightning Double-Action displayed with its description in an old Colt catalogue.

Colt model 1878 Frontier Double-Action revolvers.
Manufactured from 1878 to 1905.
Quantity manufactured: 51,210.
Available in several different calibers
including the .40-40.
Six-shot.
Closed frame.
Extractor rod on the side of the barrel.
7 ½-inch barrel (above).
4 ¾-inch barrel (right and below).

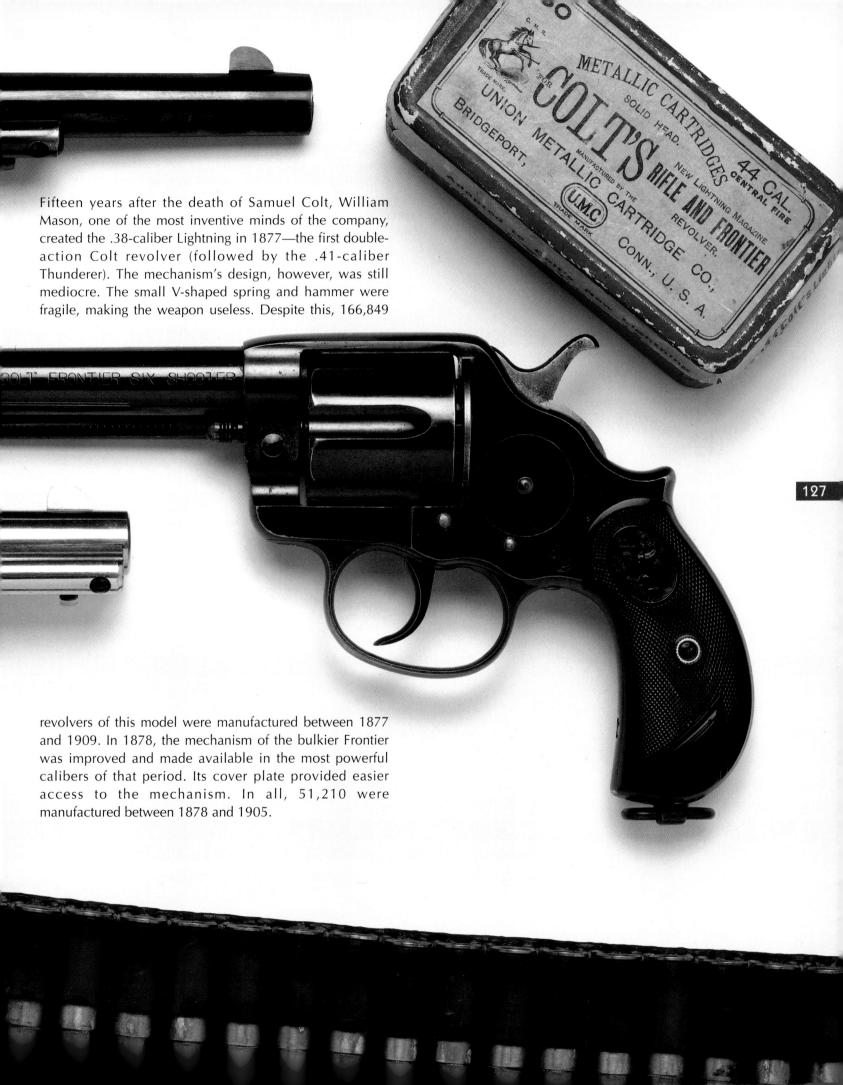

Fifteen years after the death of Samuel Colt, William Mason, one of the most inventive minds of the company, created the .38-caliber Lightning in 1877—the first double-action Colt revolver (followed by the .41-caliber Thunderer). The mechanism's design, however, was still mediocre. The small V-shaped spring and hammer were fragile, making the weapon useless. Despite this, 166,849

revolvers of this model were manufactured between 1877 and 1909. In 1878, the mechanism of the bulkier Frontier was improved and made available in the most powerful calibers of that period. Its cover plate provided easier access to the mechanism. In all, 51,210 were manufactured between 1878 and 1905.

Smith & Wesson .44 Double-Action.
Manufactured from 1881 to 1913.
Quantity manufactured: 53,668.
.44-caliber Russian.
Six-shot.
Swinging barrel and cylinder.
Simultaneous extractor.
6-inch barrel (also with 4-inch).

50 .44 CAL. S&W. RUSSIAN,
CENTRAL-FIRE CARTRIDGES
23 GRS POWDER
246 GRS BULLET
TRADE
U.M.C.
MARK
.44 S&W.
RUSSIAN
MODEL
MANUFACTURED BY
THE UNION METALLIC CARTRIDGE Co.
BRIDGEPORT, CONN., U.S.A.

Original box of 50 .44-caliber S&W Russian cartridges.

In 1880, three years after Colt, Daniel B. Wesson manufactured the first double-action S&W revolver, patented by J.H. Bullard on October 16, 1879. Production of the .38-caliber New Model, featuring break-open simultaneous extraction and available in several different barrel lengths, began in 1880. The five-shot fluted cylinder is scored with grooves on its surface. The first model (4,000 manufactured in 1880) had a cover plate whose size weakened the frame. This fault was corrected in the second model (115,000 from 1880 to 1884). On the third model (203,700 from 1884 to 1895) the grooves on the cylinder had disappeared. The trigger path was shortened and the hammer was modified in the fourth model (216,300 from 1895 and 1909). Several minor modifications were made to the fifth model (15,000 from 1909 to 1911). The .32-caliber Double-Action

Smith & Wesson .38 Double-Action
Manufactured from 880 to 1911.
Quantity manufactured: 553,000.
.38-caliber S&W.
Five-shot.
Swinging barrel and cylinder.
Simultaneous extractor.
5-inch barrel (also 3 ¼-inch).

Original box of 50 .38-caliber cartridges.

(five different models in all) was produced and developed along the same lines as the .38-caliber (327,645 manufactured between 1880 and 1919). Soon after the creation of the .38-caliber, Smith & Wesson launched a bigger .44 Double-Action, available in several different barrel lengths. From 1881 to 1913, 53,668 were

manufactured, plus 1,000 of the lighter model, the .44 Double-Action Favorite. The .38-caliber was especially successful (553,000, not including 59,400 of the .38 Double-Action Perfected Model manufactured from 1909 to 1920 with modified locking system and mechanism).

In 1887, Dan Wesson, still the active head of the company, put out a new double-action revolver with the same break-open simultaneous extraction system, but with two safety features added which, with the solid craftsmanship of this gun, ensured its success. The Safety Hammerless revolver featured an enclosed hammer and the famous safety system that makes it impossible to fire the gun unless the user holds it in his hand and pulls the trigger. It could be carried safely under one's clothes or in a pocket, without the risk of going off accidentally.

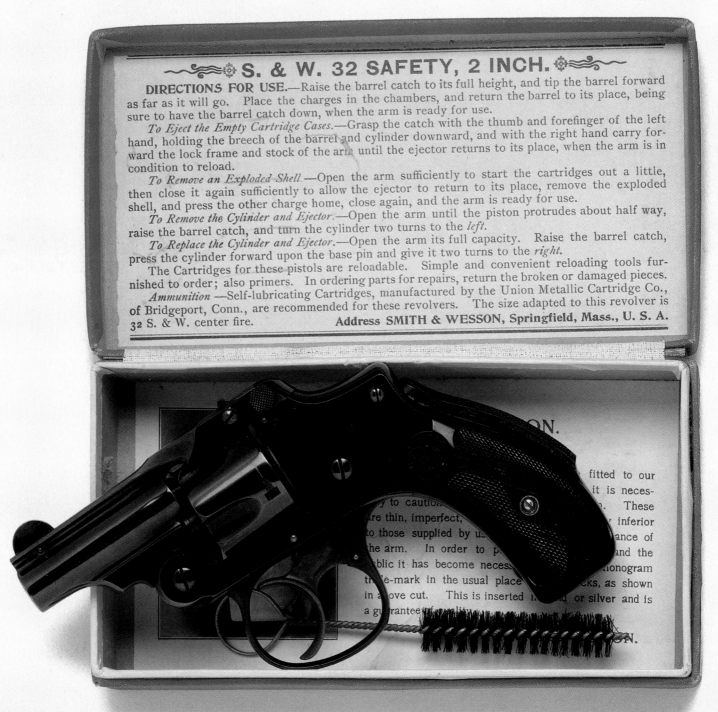

Smith & Wesson Safety Hammerless .32.
Manufactured from 1888 to 1937.
Quantity manufactured: 242,981.
.38-caliber S&W.

Five-shot.
Swinging barrel and cylinder.
Simultaneous extractor.
2-inch barrel (also 3½ inch).

Smith & Wesson Safety Hammerless .38.
Manufactured from 1887 to 1940.
Quantity manufactured: 261,493.
Double action, enclosed hammer.
.38-caliber S&W.
Five-shot.
Swinging barrel and cylinder.
Simultaneous extractor.
4-inch barrel (above).
3 ½-inch barrel (below).

From the beginning of the 1880s, arms manufacturers in Europe and the United States worked to perfect a cylinder that swung laterally outward for simultaneous extraction of spent cases and rapid reloading. In this race, Colt took the lead with its New Navy Model, which was marketed in 1889 and whose system came essentially from William Mason. This model benefitted from a marine order, hence its name. Over the years, improvements were made and a long line of guns was developed based on the 1889 Navy Double-Action: cylinder locking-notches were added on the 1892 New Army and Navy; clockwork cylinder rotation on the 1893 New Pocket, constructed on the small 'D' frame; a new Schmidt-Galand type mechanism for the .41 Frame; and, after slight modifications to the sights and finishes, it became the Army Special in 1908, which was renamed the Official Police in 1928. In production until 1969, the Official Police was Colt's best-selling revolver,

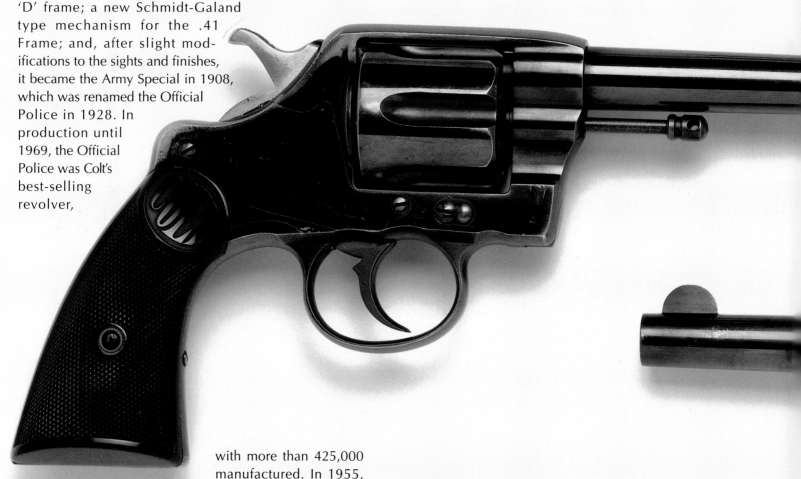

with more than 425,000 manufactured. In 1955, the famous Python was created. A new, larger frame for the New Service in 1898 replaced the New Army and Navy. The hammer safety shock-absorbing Safety Positive was part of all models made after 1905. The 1950 Cobra Model had an aluminum frame. A new frame and large helicoidal spring appeared on the MKIII models created in 1969 (this mechanism would also appear on the King Cobra and Anaconda), and the .44-caliber magnum Anaconda model appeared in 1990 with a new frame.

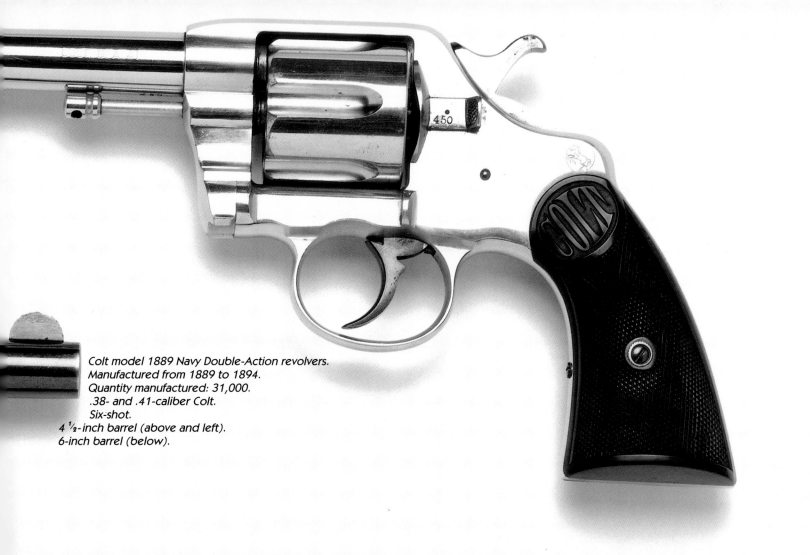

Colt model 1889 Navy Double-Action revolvers.
Manufactured from 1889 to 1894.
Quantity manufactured: 31,000.
   .38- and .41-caliber Colt.
   Six-shot.
4 ¹⁄₂-inch barrel (above and left).
6-inch barrel (below).

Descendant of wealthy Dutch settlers who had come to America in the 1600s, athlete, horseman, passionate hunter, explorer, and rancher, Theodore Roosevelt is one of America's most beloved presidents. Appointed Assistant Secretary of State for the Marines by President McKinley in 1897, he fanned the flames of the coming war with Spain, which would see America seize control of Cuba under the pretext of anticolonialism. Early on in the conflict, Roosevelt left his secretarial post in order to raise and lead a volunteer corps: the "Rough Riders," he called them, a term used in the Old West for the Texan cowboys who ran raids across the Rio Grande to fight Mexican horse thieves. Roosevelt recruited eager volunteers in New Mexico and Arizona, and patriotic students from the universities in the East, fired by nationalist fervor. The photograph opposite shows Roosevelt and his men after the bloody Battle of San Juan Hill on July 1, 1898, where a small detachment of Spanish soldiers armed with excellent Mausers held an American assault force ten times their number at bay for hours. Roosevelt distinguished himself in this battle by his disregard for danger, personally leading the attack, gun in hand. We see this revolver in his holster: a Colt 1889 Navy Double-Action, preserved in the Sagamore Hill Museum in New York, in the old Roosevelt family home.

The year 1900 marks the dawn not only of a new century, but of a new era in the history of American firearms, with the creation of the first dependable automatic pistol made in the United States, the Colt model 1900 .38 caliber. Apart from its manufacture, however, it was a Colt in name only. It had been designed by John Browning, and the four patents that he registered on April 20, 1897, were in one way or another to inspire most of the

automatic pistols that Colt was to make. Colt had already developed several different revolver cartridges (the .45, .38, and .32 Long Colt), and now went on to put the Colt name on a series for their new automatic pistol, the .45, .38, and .32 ACP (Automatic Colt Pistol), even though they had been created by Browning. At the request of the army, who were very interested in these automatics, the Colt model 1900 was manufactured in a .38 caliber, but switched to the more powerful .45 after the Philippines campaign. The breech is locked or opened by means of two barrel links, one at each end of the barrel. The slide is scored at the front for better grip while reloading (except on models ordered by the marines). Towards 1906, all models had the grooves at the rear of the slide. The Colt model 1902 can be distinguished from the 1900 by its rounded hammer spur.

Colt model 1902 Sporting Automatic Pistol.
Manufactured from 1903 to 1908.
Quantity manufactured: 7,500 approx.
Single action.
. 38-caliber ACP.
Short-recoil operating system.
Seven rounds.
Nickel finish and ivory-plated grip plates.
6-inch barrel.

Colt model 1900 Automatic Pistol.
Manufactured from 1900 to 1903.
Quantity manufactured: 3,500 approx.
Single action.
.38-caliber ACP.
Short-recoil operating system.
Seven rounds.
6-inch barrel.

Browning GP 35
Manufactured since 1935.
³/₈-inch caliber Parabellum.
Single action.
Short-recoil operating system.
13 rounds.
¹/₂-inch barrel.
Deluxe engraved model with
adjustable rear sight.

Cousin of the revolver, the automatic pistol had a different development in America than in Europe despite the fact that its most fertile and ardent developer was John Browning (1855-1926). Many remarkable guns made in Europe bear his name, although this is not the case for any of the guns he made in the United States. A number of the firearms signed by Colt, Remington, Winchester, Ithaca, or Stevens are in fact Browning's creations. The Colt .45 was a Browning, as was the Winchester 94 carbine and the Remington hunting rifle. Child of a Mormon gunsmith, Browning began learning his trade when he was just seven years old. When he was twenty four he registered his first patent, a carbine. It was bought by the Winchester Company, for whom Browning then worked for the next nineteen years. In 1890, he built a prototype of a machine gun, inventing the principle of the gas-operated firearm. This and many other of Browning's idea were bought by Colt. Browning's interest in handguns went back to 1895. At the same time as he created the Colt 1900 in America, he started producing Browning 1900 pistols for FN-Herstal in Belgium, for whom he worked until his death. Back home, his most famous pistol does not even have his name

Colt Gold Cup National Match .45.
Manufactured since 1957.
.45-caliber ACP.
Single action.
Short-recoil operating system.
Seven rounds.
5-inch barrel.
Civilian version of Colt model 1911.

on it: the Colt .45 Model 1911 Automatic Pistol, used by the American army. Between 1911 and 1970, 336,169 Colt .45s were manufactured for civilian use, and from 1911 to 1957 some 2,695,000 were made for military use, including those made under license during the Second World War. The Colt .45 is still made today in a competition model begun in 1957: the Gold Cup National Match .45. When he died, Browning was working on a $\frac{3}{8}$-inch Parabellum military pistol, which was completed posthumously as the Browning GP 35, and was used by the armies of over 50 different countries. Breaking all records for innovation in light arms, Browning triumphed over time as well: many of the pistols he created were manufactured and in use for many years after his death.

In spite of the appearance in the United States in the latter half of the twentieth century of numerous new revolver manufacturers—beginning with Ruger—two names have continued to dominate the scene: Colt and Smith & Wesson. Their preeminent position is the result of the near-perfection of their mechanisms and the remarkable quality of their manufacture. At Colt, the 1893 New Pocket revolver was improved upon in 1905 by the introduction of the Safety Positive system, with which all revolvers of this type, up to the MKIII series, created in 1969, would henceforth be equipped. The Python, sold commercially in 1955, is Colt's first post-war large frame design; it works on the same basis as the old mechanism. Constructed upon a 1908 Army Special type frame, it has

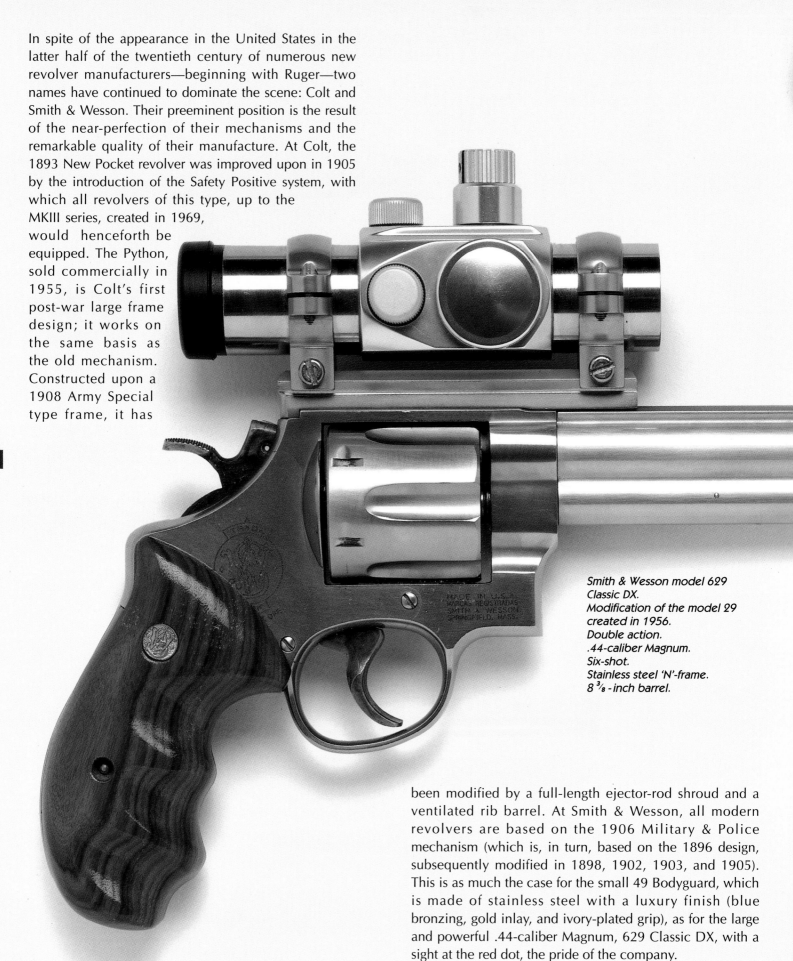

Smith & Wesson model 629 Classic DX.
Modification of the model 29 created in 1956.
Double action.
.44-caliber Magnum.
Six-shot.
Stainless steel 'N'-frame.
8 ³⁄₈ - inch barrel.

been modified by a full-length ejector-rod shroud and a ventilated rib barrel. At Smith & Wesson, all modern revolvers are based on the 1906 Military & Police mechanism (which is, in turn, based on the 1896 design, subsequently modified in 1898, 1902, 1903, and 1905). This is as much the case for the small 49 Bodyguard, which is made of stainless steel with a luxury finish (blue bronzing, gold inlay, and ivory-plated grip), as for the large and powerful .44-caliber Magnum, 629 Classic DX, with a sight at the red dot, the pride of the company.

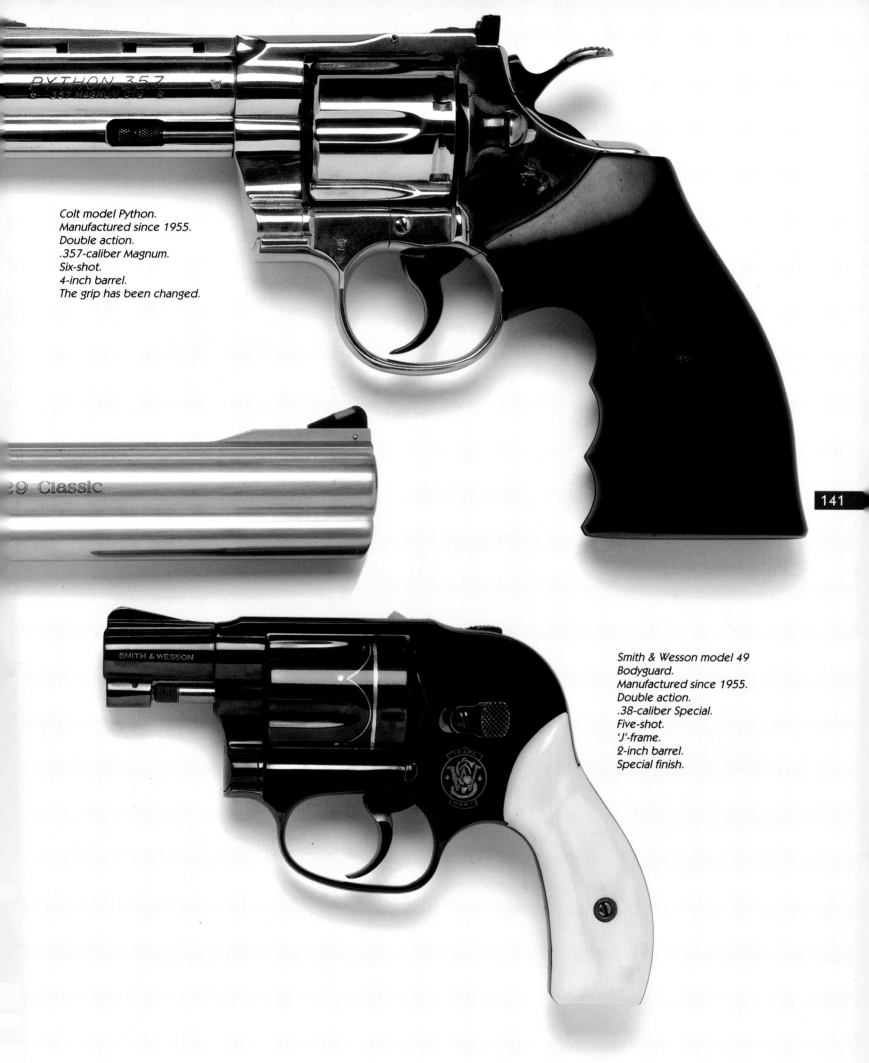

Colt model Python.
Manufactured since 1955.
Double action.
.357-caliber Magnum.
Six-shot.
4-inch barrel.
The grip has been changed.

29 Classic

141

Smith & Wesson model 49
Bodyguard.
Manufactured since 1955.
Double action.
.38-caliber Special.
Five-shot.
'J'-frame.
2-inch barrel.
Special finish.

INDEX

BIBLIOGRAPHY

Robert Elman, *Fired in Anger,* Doubleday & Co, Garden City, New York, 1968

Norm Flayderman, *Flayderman's Guide to Antique American Firearms,* DBI Books, Northfield, Illinois, 1980

Roy G. Jinks, *Smith & Wesson,* Beinfeld Publishing, North Hollywood, California, 1977

Francis A. Lord, *Civil War Collector's Encyclopedia,* Stackpole Company, Harrisburg, Pennsylvania, 1965

George Markham, *Firearms of the American Frontier, 1849-1917,* Arms and Armour Press, Londres, 1991

Harold L. Paterson, *The Remington Historical Treasury of American Guns,* Ridge Press Book, Thomas Nelson and Sons, New York, 1966

Dominique Venner, *Monsieur Colt,* Éditions André Balland, Paris, 1972

Dominique Venner, *Les Armes américaines,* Éditions Jacques Grancher, Paris, 1978

Dominique Venner, *Les Armes de poing de la nouvelle génération,* Éditions Jacques Grancher, Paris, 1982

Dominique Venner, *Les Armes qui ont fait l'histoire,* Éditions Crépin-Leblond, Paris, 1996

R. L. Wilson, *Colt, An American Legend,* Abbeville Press, New York, 1985

PHOTOGRAPHIC CREDITS

All of the photographs in this book are by Yvan Duton, with the exception of:
Private collection: pp. 42/43 ; Frederic Remington: pp. 4/5, 20/21, 96/97, 104/105, 116/117; American Information Services: pp. 6/7, 8, 134/135; Western History Collections, University of Oklahoma Library: pp. 8, 15 (above right), 28/29, 34/35, 56/57, 80/81.

The weapons in this book are part of the collections of Philippe Fossat (pp. 6/7, 26/27, 38–41, 46/47, 54/55, 60–63, 66–69, 72–79, 82–91, 94/95, 100–103, 106–109, 118–123, 126–133) and of Rudy Holst (pp. 10–15, 18/19, 22–25, 30–33, 36/37, 44/45, 48/53, 58/59, 64/65, 70/71, 92/93, 98/99, 110–115, 124/125, 136–141).

Project manager: Isabelle Raimond
Designer: Jacqueline Leymarie
Translation: Christopher Mooney, Clara Young
English edition: Cathy Muscat, Alison Bolus